PORTRAITS OF NOBEL LAUREATES IN PEACE

PORTRAITS
OF
NOBEL LAUREATES
IN
PEACE

John Wintterle and Richard S. Cramer

with photographs

ABELARD-SCHUMAN
London New York Toronto

The authors and publisher wish to thank the Nobel Foundation, Stockholm, Sweden,
for the photographs used in this book.

LONDON	NEW YORK	TORONTO
Abelard-Schuman	Abelard-Schuman	Abelard-Schuman
Limited	Limited	Canada Limited
8 King St. WC2	257 Park Ave. So.	228 Yorkland Blvd.

An Intext Publisher

Printed in the United States of America

CONTENTS

Introduction vii

1. Jean Henri Dunant: Founder of the Red Cross 1
2. Frédéric Passy: France's Apostle of Peace 7
3. Élie Ducommun: Director of the Peace Bureau 11
4. Charles Albert Gobat: Administrator Extraordinary 15
5. Sir William R. Cremer: Cofounder of the Inter-Parliamentary Union 19
6. Baroness Bertha von Suttner: Inspiration for the Peace Prize 25
7. Theodore Roosevelt: Mediation to End War 31
8. Ernesto Teodoro Moneta: Italy's Great Agitator for Peace 38
9. Louis Renault: Peace Through International Law 42
10. Klas Pontus Arnoldson: A Prophet Without Honor 45
11. Frederik Bajer: Soldier Turned Pacifist 49
12. Auguste Marie François Beernaert: Leader at The Hague Conventions 53
13. Baron d'Estournelles de Constant de Rebecque: Peace Through Diplomacy and Conventions 57
14. Tobias Michael Carel Asser: International Lawyer and Jurist 61
15. Alfred Hermann Fried: Publicist and Propagandist for Peace 64
16. Elihu Root: Peace in the Western Hemisphere 67
17. Henri Marie La Fontaine: The Last Prewar Peace Worker 71
18. Thomas Woodrow Wilson: The League of Nations 74
19. Léon Victor Auguste Bourgeois: French Leader for the League 79
20. Karl Hjalmar Branting: Socialist Pacifist for the League 82
21. Christian Louis Lange: To Preserve Peace in Time of War 86
22. Fridtjof Nansen: Explorer Turned Humanitarian 90
23. Sir Joseph Austen Chamberlain: Easing of International Tensions by Diplomacy 95
24. Charles Gates Dawes: Peace Through Financial Settlement 99
25. Aristide Briand: France and Locarno 103

26. Gustave Stresemann: Germany and Locarno   107

27. Ferdinand Buisson: World's Most Persistent Pacifist   111

28. Ludwig Quidde: Exiled Antimilitarist   114

29. Frank B. Kellogg: Treaty to Outlaw War   117

30. Nathan Söderblom: Peace Through Christianity   121

31. Jane Addams: Humanitarian and Pacifist   125

32. Nicholas Murray Butler: Peace Through Internationalism   130

33. Sir Ralph Norman Angell Lane: Peace Through the Pen   134

34. Arthur Henderson: Peace Through Disarmament   139

35. Carl von Ossietzky: Martyr for his Cause   143

36. Carlos Saavedra Lamas: Peacemaker in the Bolivia-Paraguay Chaco War   147

37. Viscount Cecil of Chelwood: Laborer for the League   150

38. Cordell Hull: Father of the United Nations   154

39. Emily Greene Balch: A Woman's Search for Peace   159

40. John R. Mott: To Ease War's Horrors   164

41. Baron John Boyd-Orr: Food for Peace   168

42. Ralph J. Bunche: Mediator Extraordinary   172

43. Léon Jouhaux: Peace Through International Labor   176

44. Albert Schweitzer: The Great Humanitarian   180

45. George C. Marshall: Reconstruction of Europe   187

46. Lester Bowles Pearson: The United Nations as Peace-Keeping Force   192

47. Reverend Dominique Georges Pire: A New Life for Refugees   199

48. Philip J. Noel-Baker: A Lifetime Search for Peace   205

49. Albert J. Luthuli: The Struggle Against *Apartheid*   208

50. Dag Hjalmar Agne Carl Hammarskjöld: Peace in the Congo   216

51. Linus Carl Pauling: The Nuclear Test Ban Treaty   223

52. Reverend Dr. Martin Luther King, Jr.: Integration Through Nonviolence   229

53. René Cassin: Defender of Human Rights   236

Appendix: Nobel Peace Prize Laureates   238

INTRODUCTION

Man is a paradox. He stands today with one foot planted on the edge of space and the other sunk deep in a primordial jungle. Creator of symphonies and cathedrals, spaceships and computers, he has given meaning to the word genocide, and has leveled cities with atomic bombs. Apparently devoted to peace, he idolizes men of war, and sometimes condemns those who would live or die for peace.

Even the founding of the Peace Prize is not without paradox; it was established by a man who amassed a fortune manufacturing dynamite and nitroglycerin, and who long believed, as he wrote to Bertha von Suttner in 1892:

> *My factories may well put an end to war sooner than your congresses. The day when two army corps can annihilate one another in one second, all civilized nations, it is to be hoped, will recoil from war and discharge their troops.*

Alfred Nobel came to realize, by 1895, that he was wrong. But what could he do to further the cause of world peace? A businessman aware of the power of money, he decided that a part of his legacy to mankind would be a cash endowment to those struggling for peace, and thus bring the cause of peace to worldwide attention.

Nobel died on December 10, 1896, leaving a simple will to govern the distribution of his fortune. It read, in part:

I, the undersigned Alfred Bernhard Nobel, hereby do declare, after mature consideration, my final will regarding the property I may leave at the time of my death to be as follows— The whole of my remaining realizable property shall be dealt with as follows:

The capital, which is to be invested by the executors in stable securities, shall constitute a fund, the annual interest on which shall be awarded as prizes to those persons who during the previous year have rendered the greatest services to mankind. The interest shall be divided into five equal parts: one part shall be awarded to the person who has made the most important discovery or invention in the realm of physics; one part to the person who has made the most important chemical discovery or improvement; one part to the person who has made the most important discovery in the realm of physiology or medicine; one part to the person who has produced the outstanding work of literature, idealistic in character; and one part to the person who shall have done the most or the best work for fraternity among nations, for the abolition or reduction of standing armies and for the holding and promotion of peace congresses.

The Peace Prize was to be awarded "by a committee of five persons to be selected by the Norwegian Storting." And Nobel continued, "It is my express wish that the prizes be distributed without regard to nationality, so that the prize may be awarded in every case to the worthiest, whether he be Scandinavian or not."

Unfortunately, Nobel drew up his will without the advice of lawyers. By the time the heirs who contested it had been paid off, and the minor bequests distributed, the original amount had been cut in half. Approximately eight million dollars remained. This, wisely invested, yields each winner in the five categories about forty-five thousand dollars.

Alfred Nobel was born on October 13, 1833, in Stockholm, Sweden. A sickly, puny boy, Alfred could not attend school, and only once, when he was eight, was he allowed in a classroom for a single year of formal schooling.

He grew to manhood in a hectic, unstable atmosphere. His father, Immanuel Nobel, a businessman and inventor, was often successful, and about as often bankrupt. Once, he even had to flee to Russia to escape his creditors. Alfred became an inventor and engineer and ultimately acquired fluency in five languages. He traveled widely and held a variety of positions. But his rise to world renown began when he returned to Sweden from Russia to help in the development of instruments of war.

Immanuel Nobel, an expert on arms, was intent upon perfecting such devices as mines and torpedoes. Looking about for a safe form of explosive, he hit upon nitroglycerin, invented some fifteen years earlier by a young Italian chemist who had considered it too dangerous to handle. Immanuel proposed to mix it with gunpowder which, when detonated, would make a powerful explosion.

Upon his return home, Alfred realized there was much to be done to make the explosive easy to use. For one thing, nitroglycerin and gunpowder nullified each other when put together, and sometimes did not work at all! He began experimenting with ways to use nitroglycerin by itself. The major problem was how to explode the substance precisely when and where it was needed. This he solved by the invention of a percussion cap, and in 1864 he received a patent covering both his cap and a detonating charge designed to be used in quarries, mines, road construction and so forth. Orders poured in for the new and powerful explosive and a small factory was founded to meet the demand. Then tragedy struck. Emil, Alfred's younger brother, and four others were killed when materials in the factory exploded.

In spite of this tragedy, in the years following, Alfred Nobel moved from triumph to triumph. The demand for his explosives never slackened and, eventually, he opened over ninety factories in the countries of Western Europe.

But with all his material success—at forty he was a multimillionaire—there is no indication that Nobel was ever a contented man. Without a family of his own, he became "Europe's richest vagabond." But where other men might have cultivated friendships and hobbies, Nobel never relaxed; rather, he used his numerous laboratories to invent ever more powerful weapons of destruction.

In the early 1870's, he bought a home in Paris and set up a laboratory. Not liking Parisian women, he advertised in foreign papers for a secretary. At a critical juncture in her life, Bertha von Suttner saw the advertisement. She applied for the position and was hired.

She met Nobel, but he was called away from Paris, and in a few days she returned home to Vienna to be married.

They did not see each other for many years. Then Bertha and her husband returned to Paris, contacted Nobel and, through him, met other members of society, many of whom were in favor of war with Germany. Not only did this inspire Bertha to write a great pacifist novel, it eventually led to Nobel's decision to do something for peace.

Ironically, Alfred Nobel, the puny, weak child, outlived everyone in his family. In 1896, the last of his brothers passed away. Alfred attended his funeral and then upon return to Paris, consulted a specialist who confirmed that he was suffering from a heart disease which, by a quirk of fate, was usually treated by minute doses of nitroglycerin!

On December 7, 1896, Alfred had a stroke, and three days later he died.

Nobel had no family; with the exception of Bertha von Suttner, he had no real friends. Yet this seeming misanthrope immortalized his name by leaving the human race one of its greatest material legacies. Five years later, in 1901, the first Nobel Prizes were awarded.

Jean Henri Dunant
Founder of the Red Cross

1828–1910

JEAN HENRI DUNANT was born in 1828 in Geneva, Switzerland, the offspring of one of Geneva's best families. His father was
a member of the governing council of the city, and his grandfather
was the director of a Geneva hospital and mayor of nearby Avully.

Socially conscious, upper-class and wealthy, the family was
also pious. So, while studying economics, in the evenings young
Henri visited the sick and suffering; on Sundays he went to church,
and then to the local prison to hold services. However, although
Dunant served for a time with the YMCA, he had been trained as

a banker, and in 1854 he entered the service of a banking firm with extensive interests in North Africa.

Four years later he struck out on his own by purchasing a large tract of land in Algeria to raise grain and beef cattle. As director and president of his own company, he invited friends and relatives to invest, which proved to be a mistake. The land needed water, and for years, he was involved in a weary and unsuccessful attempt to persuade French officials to lease him the water needed for his project.

His efforts proving futile, Dunant decided to go straight to the top, to Napoleon III, Emperor of France. However, because France was on the verge of war, he was unable to secure an audience with the Emperor. But Dunant persisted in trying and when he learned that Napoleon had left Paris to join his troops in Italy, Dunant followed him.

Traveling south in pursuit of Napoleon, Dunant reached Brescia in time to hear the roar of cannons in the distance. All the coaches had been commandeered, but he found an old oxcart and hurried onward. On the 24th of June he reached the village of Castiglione—a perfect position to observe the storm of battle.

To Dunant, safe in Castiglione, the Battle of Solferino was thrilling. The Austrian soldiers had marched all night and had gone into battle stimulated only by a double ration of schnapps. The French had been up since daybreak and, with only a few swallows of coffee, they were being asked to attack and seize positions held by an entrenched enemy.

In late afternoon, Napoleon ordered the Imperial Guard to storm Solferino and the fort of San Cassano. The assault was successful, and the Austrians were forced to retreat. The Battle of Solferino was over, but forty thousand men lay dead, dying or severely wounded.

During the battle, each side had set up field hospitals with flying pennants to guide the wounded toward help. But, confused by the colors of the pennants, artillerymen on both sides bombarded the hospitals, killing or wounding the doctors and destroying irreplaceable medical supplies.

Gradually, some order began to emerge. Word was circulated to direct or carry the wounded to Castiglione, and six thousand men poured into the little village. Every house, the small infirmary, the barracks of San Luigi, the cloister and the church of the Capuchins became a hospital. To minister to the needs of the crying, moaning, cursing mass of men were two doctors, themselves wounded and dazed.

His soul sickened by the slaughter, Dunant secured a pass from the commanding officer and hastened to the section of town where the suffering appeared the greatest. Five hundred men had fought their way into the Chiesa Maggiore, while others sprawled in front of the building. When he arrived, two Austrian prisoners were about to be thrown down the steps.

Dunant was horrified. Lifting his voice above the din, he exclaimed, "Stop. You must not! *Sono fratelli!* They are brothers!" The soldiers, amazed at the firm command, lowered their victims, and the slogan, "Sono fratelli," spread through the town.

At the Chiesa Maggiore, under Dunant's direction, vigorous activity began. Food was found, and Dunant sent his own cart to Brescia for supplies. A bandaging room was set up, and four doctors, found among the prisoners, toiled tirelessly to save the wounded and dying. A German doctor was pressed into service, as were an old naval officer, an Italian priest, a French journalist, two Italian students and two inquisitive Englishmen who had literally forced their way into the church.

In this atmosphere of pain and suffering, Dunant worked for three days and nights without sleep. He was called upon for help constantly but there was little help he could give. Instead of professionals treating the wounded, there were men who knew nothing of wounds. Where there should have been clean beds and sterile instruments, there were pallets of straw saturated with blood, pus and sweat, and crude instruments such as the saw and knife, used without anesthetic. Finally, taxed beyond endurance and exhausted, Dunant rode through the night in search of French headquarters. At six the next morning, he appeared before a French general to describe what he had witnessed at Castiglione, emphasizing the urgent need for the services of all captured Austrian doctors.

The general was impressed, and wrote a letter of introduction to the Emperor's civilian attaché at the Imperial Headquarters. Shortly after Dunant talked with the attaché, an order was issued releasing the Austrian doctors. Presumably Dunant was responsible for their liberation.

Pausing just long enough to write a letter to the charitable organizations in Geneva asking for medical supplies, Dunant continued on to Brescia and plunged into work, finding in the crude hospitals the same horror he had seen in Castiglione. In Milan a few weeks later, Dunant again filled the role of "angel of mercy" to the wounded, and here he began to toy with a new idea, one ultimately to have far-reaching implications.

In Milan, shocked by the bloodshed of the Battle of Solferino, the nobility had opened their homes to the sick and wounded, and Dunant, while ministering to the sick, began to cultivate the acquaintance of the Milanese leaders of society. As an eyewitness of the Battle of Solferino, he was in demand in the salons of the city. And there, for the first time, he discussed "the necessity of distinguishing the doctors and hospitals during a war by some emblem which would be respected by all parties." The ladies were thrilled by the idea, but the gentleman found it utopian. Men fighting wars, they said, would never respect anything as simple as an emblem.

When he returned to Geneva, Dunant was haunted by his memories of Solferino. Awake, walking, riding or just sitting quietly in his library, scenes of battle paraded before his eyes. The nights were the worst. His sleep was broken by dreams; the Chiesa Maggiore, the warm, sickly odor of blood, the moans and screams of men in torment, the dying and, worst of all, his own helplessness.

Knowing that his sanity was being stretched to the limit, he decided to write a book delineating the organization that was to be: Doctors and nurses were to be neutral, there was to be thorough preparation in case of war; natural catastrophes were to be included in the scope of the organization's activities, and an emblem or uniform was to be worn.

Almost overnight the book, *Recollections of Solferino*, became a best seller. The name of Dunant became famous. Journalists wrote articles about him and his book, and he became the social lion of the hour.

Shortly after the publication of *Recollections* a Genevan, Gustave Moynier, appeared to congratulate Dunant and to take practical steps to establish the organization. An attorney, president of the Geneva Society for Public Welfare, Moynier possessed a logical mind capable of turning an abstract idea into concrete reality. Moynier offered Dunant his support and in February, 1863, a committee met to draw up plans. Together, these men realized Dunant's dream; they founded the Red Cross.

As a result of the work of Dunant and dozens of others, an international convention was held in Geneva in 1864. There it was established that ambulances, doctors and nurses were to be regarded as neutrals in future wars, which, later, was extended to include wounded soldiers. The red cross on a white field, the inverse of the Swiss flag, was approved as the emblem of neutrality.

In 1867, three years after the convention, Dunant went bankrupt. He had spent money lavishly promoting his cause, and had paid little attention to his business. Worse than bankruptcy, he was accused of fraud. Unfortunately, he had been careless, but he had not been dishonest. Ostracized by Genevan society when he went bankrupt, and instantly cut off from all contact with the Red Cross, for a while Dunant hung on to some shreds of respectability, but gradually he faded from sight.

In 1890, he was discovered living in Lindenbuehl, Switzerland. He had become an eccentric, his health was bad, and in 1891 he entered a hospice at Heiden. There, in a home for the poor, he awaited the end.

Then, in 1895, a Swiss journalist discovered the fact that Dunant was still alive and he published an account of his meeting with the stricken old man. The story was picked up and carried in newspapers all over Europe. As a result, the Dowager Empress of Russia granted Dunant a small pension, flowers were sent by various philanthropic societies, medals were struck in his likeness and the Pope sent an inscription.

A year later, Bertha von Suttner visited Dunant. Being an editor of a magazine, she offered to publish whatever he cared to write and, through her own writing, restored him to his position as one of the world's great humanitarians.

In 1901, he was chosen to share the first Nobel Prize for Peace with Frédéric Passy. Old and ailing, Dunant could not attend the ceremonies. The Prize money he won was left untouched in a Norwegian bank. His will, probated nine years later, suggested that if the money could not be used to pay his creditors, it was to be divided between Norway and Switzerland and used for charitable purposes.

He died in 1910. The legend at the bottom of the tombstone says simply: Jean Henri Dunant, Born 1828; Died 1910. Founder of the Red Cross. Above the legend there is a carving; it shows a man kneeling and offering water to a dying soldier.

Frédéric Passy
France's Apostle of Peace

1822–1912

If BERTHA von SUTTNER, who was intimately acquainted with
Alfred Nobel, was correct, the founder of the Peace Prize did not
believe that the question of dividing the prize between two outstanding candidates would ever come up. Yet the choice of a
winner is not simple. In 1901, the year the Prize was first awarded,
it was divided between Frédéric Passy and Henri Dunant, and
through the years it has been divided many other times.

Passy was born on the 20th of May, 1822, in Paris, France.
He came from a family of bureaucrats and the family must have
had some money. Certainly Frédéric felt free, after acquiring a

degree in law, to follow a career as publicist and lecturer in political economy which, at least initially, could not have afforded him a secure income.

The origins of Passy's interest in the cause of peace are obscure. As a political economist, he was forced to contemplate the phenomenon of war and, no doubt, came to realize that war was ruinous in terms of free trade between nations. Also, Passy was a liberal and regarded war as totally destructive of the values of civilized states. As early as the 1850's he resolved, as he later wrote, to "make war on war." So in public speeches, in lectures at universities, in conversation, in such books as *Guerres et Congrés*, he stressed again and again the point that if, as Samuel Johnson put it, "Patriotism is the last refuge of scoundrels," war is the last refuge of the morally bankrupt.

Passy must be given the credit for helping put a stop to the possibility of a war between France and Germany in 1867. In that year, Napoleon III bungled an attempt to gain control of the Grand Duchy of Luxembourg. Fortunately, both governments knew they were unprepared for conflict and were willing to listen to the voice of reason. It was heard in the form of a letter written by Passy to *Le Temps*, in which he suggested the formation of a French peace society. The overwhelming response to his proposal provided Napoleon's Government with the excuse it needed to head off an immediate declaration of war.

Encouraged by public reaction to his letter, Passy and a group of friends organized the first French peace society, the Ligue Internationale et Permanente de la Paix. Passy, as secretary-general, became the guiding spirit of the society. For the next two or three years he published bimonthly articles in *Le Temps* and supervised publication of a *Bibliothèque de la Paix*, which began with one of his own works: *Conférence sur la paix et guerre*. In articles, books and pamphlets, Passy argued with all the ingenuity at his command that war between France and Germany would be catastrophic and would solve nothing.

Nevertheless war came. The French Government was intent upon the humiliation of Prussia, growing too strong on France's eastern border, and Bismarck wanted war to bring the states of southern Germany into his confederation.

For France the war *was* a catastrophe. Within a few short months, the Germans were besieging Paris. Then, as part of the peace settlement, the Germans took Alsace-Lorraine. The French vowed revenge; another handful of powder was poured into the keg that exploded in 1914.

For Passy and the League for Permanent Peace, the war was equally catastrophic. During hostilities, friends of peace must speak with muted voices. The league barely survived and, sobered by the effects of war, it ceased being a league for permanent peace. It was reorganized, after 1871, as the French Society of Friends of Peace, with Passy as president.

In the late 1880's, the British Parliament became actively interested in arbitration as a method of settling disputes between nations, and treaties were proposed between England, the United States and France. Passy, who had been elected to the Chamber of Deputies in 1881, was delighted. Securing the backing of fifty of his colleagues, he introduced into the Chamber a treaty of arbitration similar to the one proposed by the British. Naturally, the British and French treaties differed, so Passy proposed that deputies from each parliament meet in Paris to work out the details. The proposal was accepted and, in 1888, nine British and twenty-five French representatives met to confer not only about the treaty of arbitration but about matters concerning peace in general.

Although a treaty was not signed until 1903, the delegates found the problems of arbitration and peace so intricate that they decided to hold such meetings annually, and to draw in delegates from other parliaments of Europe. The Inter-Parliamentary Union was formed and, because he had been instrumental in bringing the delegates together, Passy was elected president and Sir William Cremer, the British pacifist and cofounder of the Union, was elected vice-president.

For many years, Frédéric Passy *was* the peace movement in Europe. He attended every peace conference, ran the peace society he had founded and was an active contributor to the Society's publication, *The Review of Peace*. He was the honorary president of every international peace congress, and lectured constantly for his cause. The Storting's problem of choosing a winner, or winners, in 1901 was simplified in that Frédéric had to be one of the recipients.

Despite the honor, Passy apparently had little interest in the Prize beyond the fact that it was awarded to men of peace. When some American friends visited him, shortly after the award had been given, he offered to show them the medal and the documents accompanying it. But it took his secretary a long time to find them, and Passy admitted he had not seen them since the day they arrived! It was not that he didn't feel honored; it is just that the Prize is a tribute to the activities of a single man or organization, and Frédéric Passy felt that the greatest honor the world could bestow would not be money or medals but that for which he fought —peace.

He died in Neuilly on June 12, 1912. In his last years, although blind, he kept on working. His cause was the world's cause.

Élie Ducommun
Director of the Peace Bureau

1833–1906

ÉLIE DUCOMMUN, like his friend Charles Albert Gobat (with whom he shared the Prize in 1902), won fame among peace workers as an administrator—essentially an unromantic role. However, often, when great events have been put in motion, it is the dedicated administrator and organizer who insures their continuation and gives them meaning.

In 1891, Ducommun was called upon to do an extremely difficult job. Almost single-handedly he organized, and for years was the head of, the International Peace Bureau, which served to unite the efforts of the peace workers. His selection by the Nobel

Committee of the Storting was welcomed by his colleagues who, in nominating him, clearly indicated how important they believed his achievement to be.

Ducommun was born on February 19, 1833, in Geneva, Switzerland. The family was poor (the elder Ducommun was a clockmaker), but Élie proved to be a brilliant student, and his father strained his resources to the limit to provide the boy a decent education. This, however, could not include attendance at a university, nor could Élie's father support him after he was graduated from the gymnasium. The young man who had just passed his seventeenth birthday had to find a job.

Fortunately, his search for work proved neither long nor arduous. A wealthy family in Saxony needed a tutor, and Élie's academic recommendations were so outstanding that he secured the position.

After five years as a private tutor, Ducommun returned to Geneva as a teacher in the Department of Public Instruction. However, he had hardly begun to establish himself in the school system when a powerful political figure in the Canton of Geneva offered him the management of a journal, *The Geneva Review*, which he accepted.

The position not only allowed scope for Élie's administrative talent, it brought him into contact with leading politicians. They were impressed with Ducommun and, in 1857, when he was twenty-four, he was appointed Vice-Chancellor of the Canton of Geneva. Five years later, he was promoted to Chancellor!

To have attained this position at such an early age would have gratified most men, but Ducommun was not satisfied with his career. In 1865, he founded and edited a paper called *Progress*. A few years later, even though the paper was successful, he left to become the editor of another journal in Bern.

In Bern, as in Geneva, his editorial activities brought him into contact with important men in politics and business and, in 1873, the board of directors of the Jura-Simplon Railroad offered him the position of secretary-general. He accepted, remaining with the railroad until just before his death in 1906.

Probably, Ducommun first became interested in the peace movement because he was convinced that the future of Europe lay in political and economic unity and that unity was impossible without peace. As early as 1868, he took upon himself the task of editing the French edition of a newspaper entitled *Les États-Unis d'Europe*, founded in Paris and supported by the Ligue Internationale de la Paix et de la Liberté. He also attended various peace congresses.

But it was not until the third meeting of the International Peace Conference, which met in Rome in 1891, that Ducommon emerged as one of the outstanding peace advocates in Europe. At this conference, a proposal emerged, and was accepted, for the creation of an international peace bureau. The necessity for such a bureau was obvious, but it was less obvious who was to be appointed director and where it was to be established.

Switzerland, with its long history of peaceful neutrality, was the logical choice as to location, and Élie Ducommun, who was known to many of the delegates as a splendid administrator, was the choice for the post of secretary.

Though his position with the Jura-Simplon Railroad kept him busy, Ducommon could not refuse. He did impose one condition; he would receive no salary! The delegates were aware of the magnitude of the task assigned Ducommun, but there was little money for the cause of peace and they accepted his condition.

When the bureau began to function on December 1st, 1891, Ducommun was without secretarial help and could give only his spare hours to its activities. Yet his achievements were astonishing. Besides carrying on a large correspondence with the leading peace advocates in the major countries of the Western world, he initiated the collection and classification of everything, in any country or language, that dealt with the question of peace. He brought together the archives of the various peace organizations; he sent out, in the name of all the organizations, statements of their activities; he prepared the agendas of the peace conferences that met every year; he published a number of brochures explaining the purpose of the peace movement; and he founded and edited a bimonthly magazine dealing with peace. In reviewing what was only a partial list of his accomplishments Frédéric Passy referred to Ducommun as "incomparable."

On the morning of December 10, 1902, to the surprise of nobody but Ducommun, he received a telegram informing him that he had been selected to share one of the world's most coveted prizes. The man, who had for so many years labored for peace and refused all awards, at last found one he could not refuse: the admiration of the world.

As might be expected, the Prize money went to further the cause of peace. He considered the world's admiration was more than enough for everything he had done or tried to do. His colleagues did not agree. On his seventieth birthday he was honored with a huge dinner party and with a gift of money donated by all the international peace organizations.

Three years later, on December 7, 1906, he died in Bern, Switzerland.

Charles Albert Gobat
Administrator Extraordinary

1843–1914

CHARLES ALBERT GOBAT was born on May 21, 1843, in Jura, Switzerland. The family was well-to-do, and so Charles was encouraged to attend the universities of Basle, Bern and Heidelberg where, having proved himself a brilliant student, he was awarded the degree of doctor of laws in 1865.

Normally, with a degree of doctor of laws, an individual settles down to legal practice or he becomes a teacher. Gobat did neither. His interest in philosophy, literature and law unsatiated, he moved to the College de France and the Sorbonne for postdoctoral work.

In 1865, he returned to Switzerland, established himself as an advocate in Bern and became *privat-docent* of French civil law at the university. He was successful both as a lawyer and a lecturer. A large, powerfully built man, filled with passionate energy that spilled over into his actions and speech, he was convincing in argument and as witty in debate as he was expert in law. His only undesirable characteristic was an abruptness of manner that was often mistaken for arrogance; but it was more the result of a quick mind that reached a conclusion while a question was being asked.

Despite his success in Bern, Gobat was not content. He was interested in politics and the political life of the city was dominated by well-entrenched politicians. Casting about for a town offering a wider scope for his ambitions, he decided upon Delemont, close enough to be almost a suburb of Bern. There, sometime before 1870, he opened a law office.

Success came with unprecedented swiftness and, by 1880, he had become one of the most noted advocates in the region. He had made himself an authority in the field of education and had been elected to a series of minor offices, which led to his becoming a power in cantonal politics. His reward came in 1882 when he was not only elected to the Grand Council of Bern and called to a seat on the State Council, but also was appointed Superintendent of the Department of Public Instruction—a position he was to hold for the next twenty-four years.

Gobat was extremely effective as a superintendent of education. In his dual role of educator and politician, he was one of the promoters of federal subsidies for commercial education and for the study of the fine arts. He promoted a revision of the Primary Education Act, and he instituted a reform of secondary education which reduced the years devoted to Latin and Greek in favor of modern languages and natural sciences. He prevailed upon the University of Bern to create several extension courses for adult education and to him goes the credit for promoting the building program that made Bern a great university.

It is not clear why Gobat became interested in international peace. However, having been elected to the Swiss Federal Council in 1890, he led the Swiss delegation to the third session of the Inter-Parliamentary Union, held in 1891.

Gobat proved to be an effective member of the Inter-Parliamentary Union and, at the close of the session in Rome, he was called upon to organize the next session in Bern and to act as the presiding officer. When the union met in 1892, it held its meetings for the first time on the premises of a national parliament, the Bundespalast.

One of the problems that the Bern conference had to grapple with was the lack of coordination of effort. With the exception of the annual conference, there was little contact between the various delegations. Also, only twelve nations participated in the conference and, since the strength of the union must rest upon the number of participating members, active propaganda work was necessary to establish a union in as many countries of the world as possible. Finally, someone, or some group, was needed to organize the conference each year, rather than, as in the past, leave the question to a vote of the delegates.

After lengthy debate, it was decided to establish the Inter-Parliamentary Bureau and to appoint Charles Albert Gobat as its first secretary-general. From 1892 till 1909, when the bureau was moved to Brussels, he remained its head.

During these seventeen years Gobat labored arduously in the cause of world peace. He carried on a huge correspondence with individual members of the IPU, keeping each national group informed of what the others were doing. He made the arrangements for the annual conferences and did all the work that goes into holding successful gatherings. In addition, between 1893 and 1897, he served as chief editor of the union's monthly review, *La Conférence Interparlementaire*, and published a brief history of the union.

During those same years, Gobat was Superintendent of the Department of Public Instruction for the Canton of Bern and a member of the Swiss equivalent of the House of Representatives (where for years he carried on a fight to have the principle of arbitration adopted), and he also managed to write a two-volume history of Switzerland.

In 1902, he was nominated for the Nobel Peace Prize. Unaware that he was even being considered, the telegram announcing that he had been chosen to share the Prize with his countryman, Élie Ducommun, came as a pleasant shock. Even more gratifying to him was the worldwide recognition of the work of the Bureau that followed the award.

In the years after 1902, as the armaments race in Europe brought war ever closer, Gobat's role in the struggle for peace became even greater. He published extensively in journals dedicated to peace, and in the more popular journals read by the rank and file of people who did not want war, but were unfamiliar with the arguments against it, and with what was being done to prevent it. He occupied a leading position at all the peace conferences and published reports of the proceedings. In 1904, he led a Swiss delegation to an Inter-Parliamentary Union Conference held in St. Louis, Missouri, and was the spokesman of the group that presented a petition asking President Roosevelt to convene a second governmental international peace conference.

In 1906, when his friend Élie Ducommun died, Gobat succeeded him as director of the International Peace Bureau, a world center for unofficial pacifist propaganda. Thus, until the headquarters of the Inter-Parliamentary Union was moved to Brussels in 1909, he was simultaneously director of the two largest peace organizations in the world.

Only a man as dedicated as Charles Albert Gobat could have filled his many difficult roles so satisfactorily. But his unceasing efforts in the cause of peace took their toll. On March 16, 1914, he collapsed during a meeting of the International Peace Bureau and died.

Sir William R. Cremer

Cofounder of the Inter-Parliamentary Union

1838–1908

The future Member of Parliament and peace delegate to the world, William Cremer, was born on March 18, 1838, at Farnham, Hampshire, England. His parents were poor and his father deserted the family shortly after William's birth, leaving his wife with the responsibility of providing for the baby and two older daughters.

Mrs. Cremer was qualified to run a village school, and earned very little money—just enough to keep the children alive. However, in later years, one of William's most vivid memories was of being perpetually hungry as a child.

After learning his letters at his mother's knee, William attended school for a short time but, at the age of twelve, he had to get a job and help support the family.

The only kind of work William could find was manual labor. He became a pitch boy in a shipyard—carrying buckets of pitch from a bubbling caldron to men calking the seams of a vessel. The job paid two shillings, the equivalent of about fifty cents, for a seventy-two-hour work week. He learned what it was like to rise before dawn, to fumble his way into tattered clothing and join long lines of men making their way down to the docks to begin the day's work. He knew what it was like to be an apprentice in the building trade, to work for little pay, to be always at the mercy of his master. The welfare of the working man remained a major concern for the rest of his life, and later he became one of the most powerful labor leaders in England.

In 1859, Cremer participated in one of the fiercest labor conflicts in English history. Carpenters and joiners had been agitating for a nine-hour day and a decent wage. Unable to force employers to heed their demands, they threatened to organize; if necessary, to strike. The employers refused to negotiate and locked up their businesses to starve the workers into submission.

Contrary to the expectations of the employers, the workers, led by the twenty-one-year-old Cremer and six other men refused to give up. They organized into the Amalgamated Society of Carpenters and Joiners and continued to fight bitterly for their goals.

Eventually the labor dispute was settled by negotiation. The workers gave up part of their demands, employers met them halfway on others, and the men went back to work. For the young labor leader, the long struggle served as a revelation. The men had suffered terribly for six months, while the strike went on. How much more sense it would have made if negotiations had started before the strike began!

What was true of labor relations, he thought, was true of nations. Wars are usually generated by the unleashed passions of the participants, and the involved nations frequently scorn the thought of negotiation. Since any war anywhere affects all mankind, Cremer felt that nations refusing to negotiate with each other should be forced by law to arbitrate their difficulties.

However, no such laws existed. The desire for conflict had to be changed, and that could only be done via the path of neutrality and propaganda.

In 1870, when the Franco-Prussian War began, Cremer seized his opportunity. Convinced that England must stay out, he formed a committee of fifty men to appeal to the working class to support a policy of neutrality. Due partially to the committee's efforts, but primarily because she considered her vital interests were not affected, England did not get involved.

With Germany's eventual victory, the committee did not disband. It grew into the Workman's Peace Association. As secretary and guiding spirit, Cremer had the responsibility of keeping the Association afloat economically. He succeeded, and gradually the association grew in membership.

By 1875, the organization was secure enough to expand its activities to the international level. Its name was changed to the International Arbitration League, and plans were devised to establish chapters in the major nations of the West. The league was to exist solely for the purpose of promoting the concept of international arbitration.

The league had barely been established when war broke out again, this time between Russia and Turkey, a war in which British interests *were* threatened. Portions of the press clamored for war, the people were inflamed and the Cabinet was prepared. The cause of peace was unpopular, but Cremer was adamantly opposed to British intervention. In the fall and winter of 1876-77, he collected and presented to the Government the signatures of over three hundred officers of various trade unions opposing intervention. It is difficult to measure the effect of the petition, but thanks to the work of Cremer and others, the opponents of war had begun to organize.

The years of Cremer's struggle for peace followed his election to Parliament as one of twelve labor MP's, in 1885. Until his death in 1908, he was in a position to command not only the attention of the working classes but that of the Government, since it was aware that he represented the muted voices of hundreds of thousands of workers.

In 1887, Cremer had been introduced to Andrew Carnegie, an American multimillionaire and advocate of peace, who was as interested as Cremer was in the principle of arbitration. Carnegie attended an International Arbitration League meeting, at Cremer's invitation, was impressed by the work being done and thereafter assisted the league with money and influence. At the league meeting, Carnegie held lengthy discussions about the possibility of working out a treaty of arbitration between the two great democracies. Cremer was most enthusiastic. A memorial drawn up by Cremer embracing the concept of arbitration was accepted by the House of Commons, then presented to the President of the United States, Grover Cleveland. The document in no way bound the President, so he accepted it, and the United States Congress passed a resolution in favor of arbitration. With both nations acknowledging the principle, only the details of an arbitration treaty remained to be worked out.

However, this proved to be an insurmountable barrier. Despite Cremer's most valiant efforts, in 1897, a multitude of obstacles led the United States Senate to reject a carefully constructed arbitration treaty.

It was a crushing blow for the friends of peace, but their work continued. Treaties of arbitration were signed between England and a dozen other countries, including France, in 1903. But the abstention of the most powerful nation in the world tended to vitiate the work done simply because any action of the United States in terms of peace or war could so easily be decisive.

Of all the organizations, societies and peace movements with which Cremer was associated during the last forty years of his life, the most important was the Inter-Parliamentary Union, brought into being by Passy in 1888. In recognition of his work for arbitration, Cremer was elected first vice-president, and then secretary —a position he was to hold for the rest of his life.

As secretary, Cremer shouldered the entire responsibility for the success or failure of the organization and also most of the work. At the London conference in 1890, Cremer's foresight in handling local arrangements made it a resounding success. Such topics as peace, disarmaments and arbitration were discussed and, while no conclusive results were achieved, the intricate problems involved were thoroughly reviewed and the foundation laid for solid achievements in the future.

The union continued to meet frequently in various cities of Europe. In 1894, in Amsterdam, it took another epoch-making step which resulted in the establishment of a Permanent International Court of Arbitration at The Hague in 1899.

However, the world's nations were now engaged in an armaments race and rarely in history have nations so engaged not gone to war. Cremer realized the danger. Again and again in Parliament, he denounced the emphasis upon armaments. In 1907, old and tired, his health failing, he made one last great effort to avert the tragedy he saw coming. On his own initiative, he drew up a fraternal address, secured the signatures of three thousand trade-union leaders and forty-eight labor MP's, and presented it to German workers. Pointing out there was no cause for war, he concluded by calling for a meeting between British and German workers, to be held in Berlin.

The meeting was held, but it was ineffectual. Then, in the second week of July, 1908, Cremer caught pneumonia. He died on July 22.

Glancing back over Cremer's career, one discovers no rattle of drums, no playing for stakes involving the life and death of nations, nothing but endless conferences. But Cremer's cause was the continued existence of civilization itself.

The Nobel Committee recognized his worth. In 1903, he was awarded the Nobel Prize for Peace. The Arbitration League, proud of the man who had led it for so many years, gave him a dinner, and in the speech that followed Cremer announced that the money would be used to set up an endowment trust for the

International Arbitration League. The interest accruing from the fund would, he hoped, enable the officers to further the work of the league.

William Cremer was knighted by King Edward VII in 1907, a tribute to his stature in English political life. But a greater tribute is to be found in a note written by Andrew Carnegie at the time of Cremer's death:

> *Cremer was the ideal of the twentieth-century hero; the hero of civilization as contrasted with that of the barbarous past— the man who devotes his life to "serve or save his fellows," in contrast to him who kills or maims them. Truly I know of no final, more heroic life than that of Cremer. It should be held up for the imitation of men.*

Baroness Bertha von Suttner

Inspiration for the Peace Prize

1843–1914

No more unlikely candidate for a Nobel Prize could have been found than Bertha von Suttner. Descendent of an ancient and distinguished Austrian military family, she was born Bertha Sophia Felicite, Countess Kinsky, on June 8, 1843, in Prague. Her father, who died before her birth, had been a field marshal in the Austrian Army, and her mother was descended from the Austrian nobility.

Descriptions of her early years picture her as a highly intelligent, charming, fun-loving girl with a real talent for music and languages. Hers might well have been the story of a sheltered, pampered young woman who enjoyed all the advantages in youth, married well and continued to enjoy them, had it not been for her mother's gambling fever. This mania carried her mother, accompanied by her daughter, on trips to Wiesbaden, Baden-Baden and other gambling resorts. By herself, Bertha visited Italy and briefly studied music in Paris and Milan. When money for further study and gambling came to an end, the young girl had to find work.

Until the family finances were exhausted, Bertha had moved in the best social circles, and she had met a number of outstanding men and women in Europe. Although her voice was not good enough for concert singing, she had received a thorough grounding in music and had become fluent in several languages.

The ways in which a young woman could be self-supporting were limited in the 1870's. However, Bertha found a position as instructor and companion to four daughters in the baronial house of von Suttner in Vienna.

By the standards of that day, when she went to the von Suttners, Bertha was almost an old maid. She had had a fair share of romance in her life, and had been engaged three times but never married.

However, the von Suttners had a twenty-three-year-old son, Arthur, who found Bertha as attractive at thirty as other men had at twenty, and he fell in love. The romance blossomed. The girls found out and were delighted. The parents found out, and were not. For the son of a baron to court a governess was not acceptable.

So the old baroness and the countess had a talk one afternoon. The embarrassment of the situation was relieved by Bertha's awareness that the match was impossible, and that she could not stay on as governess in the von Suttner family.

The countess had noticed an advertisement in a newspaper which read: "A rich, cultured, elderly gentleman, living in Paris, desires to find a mature lady, familiar with languages, to act as secretary and manager of his household." Bertha wrote to the gentleman explaining that she read and wrote French, German and English. His reply indicated interest in Bertha's application and, after a further exchange of letters, she was hired. She arrived in Paris knowing little about her employer except that he was Alfred Nobel, the inventor of dynamite.

She found him to be a cultured gentleman. He, in turn, found the countess vivacious and charming, and a friendship was established that was to last until Nobel died.

But a week after her arrival in Paris, Nobel was called home to Sweden and during his absence Bertha received the following telegram from Arthur, "I cannot live without you." She wrote Nobel informing him she could not—after all—accept the position, pawned her last piece of jewelry, and caught a train to Vienna. Upon arrival, she sent Arthur a note to meet her, and they decided to get married immediately.

With the wrathful vengeance of Baron and Baroness von Suttner hanging over their heads, they were married in a little parish church. But they could not stay in Vienna so they accepted an invitation to honeymoon in Mingrelia, a Caucasian principality. Happy and safe in Mingrelia, they wrote the elder von Suttners and found them cold and unforgiving.

The newlyweds could not be guests forever. They moved first to Kutais, the chief city of Mingrelia, and then to Tiflis. There, Bertha gave music lessons and Arthur found a position as a bookkeeper. To supplement their income, both began to publish quite extensively.

Arthur was the first to get into print. During the Russian-Turkish war of 1877, he wrote articles describing the home front, life in the Caucasus and their travels, all of which were accepted by magazines and newspapers in Vienna. Encouraged by his success, Arthur influenced Bertha to write also. Dashing off a short, light essay she sent it to the Vienna *Presse*. To her astonishment, she promptly received a letter of acceptance and a check for twenty florins.

It was the beginning of a new career. In the months following, Bertha wrote and published a number of short stories and articles. Then, with Arthur, she published a novel that was modestly successful. Together, they wrote several other novels, but their dream of becoming independent through writing did not materialize.

The question of earning a living soon ceased to be a problem. The elder von Suttners, who had refused a reconciliation when Arthur and Bertha were married, softened as the years passed and, in 1885, the prodigal couple returned to Vienna. Two years later, they made a trip to Paris where, after eleven years, Bertha again met Alfred Nobel.

Nobel hadn't been at all dismayed by Bertha's abrupt departure. They had exchanged letters while she and Arthur were in the Caucasus; now their friendship was renewed.

Bertha found Nobel little changed by the years. He was slightly grayer, more absorbed in his work, more melancholy, but still the perfect host and splendid conversationalist. He invited Bertha and Arthur to his home, showed them his library and his laboratory, and took them to the salon of Madame Juliette Adam, a society leader who used her position to urge revenge upon Germany for the humiliations France had suffered in the Franco-Prussian War.

In Madame Adam's salon, the baroness found, to her shocked disgust, that the hostess and her friends actively wanted war. In a short seventeen years they had forgotten the horror of the siege of Paris—the deaths, the mutilations, the starvation and the rioting in the streets.

Something, Bertha thought, had to be done to balance the activities of people like Madame Adam. Somehow she had to cut through all the verbiage about honor and glory and demonstrate that war is shoddy, and is the product of sick minds. She had one weapon; she could write.

Bertha decided to write a novel. She talked to men who had been in battle, who had felt shrapnel tearing into their bodies or the rip of a bayonet. She talked to army surgeons and read their reports. She interviewed field officers who described how men looked when they were dying. She extended her research into libraries and archives, reading and taking notes on the most recent campaigns.

Months later, she finished writing one of the most influential novels of the nineteenth century. A novel so powerful, so biting in its indictment of war that the editor of a leading German periodical—who had always before accepted her manuscripts—refused to publish it. Her publisher finally agreed to bring out *Die Waffen Nieder (Lay Down Your Arms)* only because of their contract. The publisher had made a wise decision. Within a decade, the book had been translated into twelve languages and had sold over a million and a half copies.

The immediate effect of the book made the baroness famous overnight, and put her in touch with the various peace societies of Europe. In 1891, the Inter-Parliamentary Union (IPU) was to hold its first annual meeting in Rome. There was some question whether Italian members of Parliament would attend. The baroness managed to secure the cooperation of the Italian government, and then found that her own Austrian government wasn't participating.

Returning to Vienna, she set to work to remedy the situation. In spite of protests that the moment wasn't right for Austria to participate, the baroness managed to reach several sympathetic deputies in the Reichsrath. As a result, a creditable delegation was sent to the Inter-Parliamentary meeting.

Then it occurred to Bertha that if a peace congress were held in Rome at the same time as the IPU meeting, it would strengthen the peace movement. She found, however, that Austria had no peace society to send delegates to such a congress. Obviously, there was only one thing to do: establish the society.

On September 3, 1891, she published a peace appeal in the *Neue Freie Presse.* The response was overwhelming. Hundreds of letters poured in indicating support and sympathy. Satisfied that the necessary backing would be forthcoming, she founded the Austrian Peace Society, with a membership roll of two thousand, most of whom had read her novel.

In the years following, Baroness von Suttner became a leader in the peace movement. At the fourth World Peace Congress held in Bern, Switzerland in 1892, she met Nobel and began urging him to do something for the cause of peace. "Inform me, convince me," he said, "and then I will do something great for the movement." She tried, and it is generally agreed that she was instrumental in persuading him to establish the Peace Prize.

That same year the journal *Die Waffen Nieder* was established with Bertha as editor and she was also active in helping form the German Peace Society.

Four years later, her friend Alfred Nobel died. Shortly before his death he had written to Bertha, "I am enchanted to see that the peace movement is gaining ground."

The baroness was not among the first to win the Prize. Passed over six times, she finally received the coveted telegram informing her she had been chosen, on December 10, 1905.

The sixty-two-year-old baroness was exhausted when news of the award came and she accepted it *in absentia*. Her magnificent vitality had been impaired by the death of her beloved husband in 1902. Almost overnight she changed from a vivacious, middle-aged woman to an old one. However, her cause was greater than her personal grief; and in work she found relief from the memories of twenty-five years of almost perfect marriage. She finally journeyed to Norway in the spring of 1906 to deliver her acceptance speech.

As the winner of a Nobel Prize, she was now doubly famous. Each year found her on a speaking tour, or attending conferences; and each year her tongue grew sharper. For many who felt the lash of her words directly or by implication, she became, not as she had earlier been called, *Friedensbertha* (Peace-Bertha), but *Friedensfurie* (Peace-fury). But for those who worked with her, she was the "angel of peace."

In 1912, after a speaking tour in the United States, the baroness returned to Europe. Old and tired, she collapsed while speaking at a public meeting in Vienna. She needed an operation, but refused to have one. She was seventy-one and thought her life's work was done. A month later, on June 20, 1914, she died. On August 1st, Germany declared war on Russia.

Theodore Roosevelt
Mediation to End War

1858–1919

On October 27, 1858, a future President of the United States was born in New York City. The second of four children, Theodore Roosevelt was a delicate child who suffered from asthma. Fortunately for the young boy, his father was a banker who could afford the best in doctors, nurses and governesses, as well as private tutors and trips abroad.

Theodore passed into his teens a tall, slender boy with thin arms and legs. Not aware of being extremely nearsighted, he read constantly, doing further damage to his eyes. At the age of thirteen, he was given a gun for his birthday and was amazed when his companions shot at things that he couldn't even see. He had his eyes tested and shortly thereafter began to wear glasses.

A sickly youth, with little physical strength, Teddy was unable to hold his own with other boys. But when he was fourteen, an incident occurred that set him on the road to strength and health. Suffering from an attack of asthma, he was sent to a resort in the mountains. On the stagecoach, he was pestered by a couple of boys his own age. Angered, Theodore tried to fight them and discovered that either of his opponents could handle him with ease. Determined to avoid such humiliation in the future, he learned to box and lift weights. In later years, when he was President, he was still boxing, riding, wrestling and practicing judo.

As an undergraduate at Harvard, Roosevelt was a good student. Beginning with his freshman year, he maintained a fairly rigid schedule. Getting up at 7:15 in the morning, he spent the day at his books or in class. On Saturday he studied about six hours. As a result, he graduated on June 30, 1880, twenty-first in a class of over a hundred, high enough to be admitted to Phi Beta Kappa.

A week before Theodore's twentieth birthday, he fell in love with Alice Hathaway Lee. "I first saw her on October 18, 1878," he wrote, "and loved her as soon as I saw her sweet, fair young face." They were married in 1880. He was twenty-two and had just been graduated from college, and Alice was nineteen.

In his last years in college, Roosevelt decided to study law. Enrolling in Columbia Law School, he was soon bored to distraction. Almost by accident, he joined the Republican party and shortly found himself a candidate for the state legislature. He had discovered his real career—politics.

His nomination to the legislature resulted from a fight between two Republican bosses, Joe Murray and Jake Hess. The contest was to see who could get the most men elected to the state legislature. Joe Murray felt that Roosevelt would be a good candidate to run in the Twenty-first, "the silk-stocking," District in New York. He was right. Roosevelt's friends voted for him, and Joe saw to it that the lower economic class did also. Theodore won his first elective office.

During his second term in the legislature, Roosevelt suffered a double tragedy that had a terrible impact on his life. In the summer of 1883, Alice learned she was going to have a baby. When the time for the delivery grew near, the young couple moved in with Theodore's mother so Alice would have company while he was away in Albany. On February 13, after spending all day in the legislature, Roosevelt learned that his wife had given birth to a daughter.

He hurried home, only to find Alice could hardly recognize him. Holding her body in his arms, he sat through the endless hours of the night. At 3 A.M. he was informed that his mother had just died of typhoid fever. At two o'clock the following day, Alice died of Bright's disease. The two deaths temporarily ended what had been a most promising political career.

But as Roosevelt remarked to his son, Ted, at a later date, "I rose like a rocket," in the legislature. By 1884, he had become so important that he was nominated for Speaker of the House. But, being a reformer, he had antagonized too many powerful figures by his forthright honesty and was defeated in the next election.

After spending a few years as a rancher in the Dakota badlands, Roosevelt returned to New York, both to marry Edith Kermit Carow and to reenter politics. He ran for mayor and was defeated, but when the Republican Benjamin Harrison was elected President, Roosevelt accepted an appointment to the United States Civil Service Commission.

His subordinates' introduction to Roosevelt was a loud bustle in the outer office, the door opening with a crash, and Roosevelt bounding in. "I am the new Civil Service Commissioner. Have you a telephone? Call up the Ebbitt House. I have an engagement with Archbishop Ireland. Say I will be there at ten o'clock." The new boss was an earnest, dynamic man who got things done, loved a good fight, attacked immorality wherever he found it, and rendered a tremendous service for his country by drawing attention to civil service reform.

By 1895, Roosevelt was convinced he had done all he could as Civil Service Commissioner and accepted a position as commissioner of the New York City Police Board. There, as on the Civil Service Commission, he proved to be a flamboyant figure and a good subject for reporters in search of a story. On his first day as commissioner he rushed into headquarters and demanded, "What'll we do now?"

On hot summer days, he wore a pink silk shirt with a black sash around his waist, and a black, wide-brimmed hat. At night, wrapped in a long, black cloak, he roamed the streets checking up on his officers. Endowed with large, shiny white teeth, Roosevelt was the delight of cartoonists. They pictured him slinking down dark streets, frightening policemen by chattering his teeth at them or, if they were not doing their duty, they were shown cowering in terror before a set of gleaming molars.

In 1897, Roosevelt was ready to move on. William McKinley had just been elected President and offered Teddy the position of Assistant Secretary of the Navy.

Roosevelt accepted. It was a crucial moment in American history. The United States had been having trouble with Spain over Cuba, and then, on February 14, 1898, the battleship *Maine* was sunk in Havana's harbor. The American people were led to believe that Spain was responsible for the sinking and demanded war. "Remember the *Maine*" became a battle cry. President McKinley came under terrible pressure and, on April 11, 1898, he asked Congress for a declaration of war.

At the Navy Department, as war hysteria had mounted between February and April, Roosevelt was champing at the bit. He wanted the Navy to do all kinds of things to prepare for war. But he was responsible to his chief, Secretary John Davis Long, and couldn't give orders. One day when Long decided to take an afternoon off and rest, for a few brief hours, Roosevelt was in charge and, in typical Roosevelt fashion, he began doing things.

The next day, the Secretary of the Navy noted in his diary, "The very devil had seemed to possess Roosevelt." He had ordered ships hither and yon, had ordered supplies and ammunition, and all but called up the reserves. He had sent a telegram to George Dewey, admiral of the Asiatic Fleet, who was resting in

Hong Kong, informing him to coal his ships and, in case war was declared, to make sure the Spanish squadron did not leave the Asiatic coast. Actually, as a result of this cable, Dewey was in a position to attack the Spanish fleet in Manila Bay and his victory gave the United States possession of the Philippine Islands.

With the country at war, there was every justification for Roosevelt to remain at his post in the Navy, especially since his wife and one of his sons were ill. But men were being recruited, and he found he could not sit by idly and watch. So he solicited a commission as lieutenant colonel of a volunteer cavalry regiment.

In the Cuban campaign, Roosevelt was extremely brave and extremely reckless. Mounted on horseback, dashing here and there shouting encouragement, and leading his famous charge up San Juan Hill, he was, without doubt, the *most* colorful figure in the war.

Returning from the Cuban campaign a hero, Roosevelt found himself in demand as a politician. The Republican bosses in New York needed a man to run for governor, and Roosevelt was the obvious choice. He accepted the nomination and, after a hard fight, won by the slim margin of some eighteen thousand votes.

While Teddy Roosevelt cannot be considered the greatest governor New York has ever had, he was a good one. But as a reform governor, he antagonized powerful political bosses, even those who had engineered his election. So, in 1900, the political bosses of New York manipulated his nomination for Vice-President and Roosevelt reluctantly accepted. It was a fortunate choice. On September 6, 1901, President McKinley was shot, and he died in Buffalo on September 14. At three o'clock on the afternoon of the 15th, Roosevelt took the oath of office and became the 26th President of the United States.

Teddy Roosevelt gained extreme popularity and no one familiar with his presidential career can deny the magnitude of his achievements. From helping to promote a revolution in Panama —which gave the United States control of the Canal Zone—to actively promoting the Pure Food and Drug Act, little escaped his eye or was outside the scope of his attention.

It was while he was President that Roosevelt performed the meritorious service that won him the Nobel Prize for peace despite his own earlier record. The Prize was bestowed because he helped to stop the Russo-Japanese War of 1904.

On February 8, 1904, without a declaration of war, Japan attacked the Russian fleet off Port Arthur and won a decisive victory. Then, Japan amazed the world by her successes on both land and sea. A revolution in Russia in 1905, together with heavy losses, sapped Russia's will to fight and it appeared as though Japan might win. However, by the middle of 1905 Japan was exhausted and could not prolong the war. Both sides were willing to consider peace.

Roosevelt secretly applauded the efforts of the Japanese, but believed the interests of the United States in the Far East would be best served if a balance of power between Russia and Japan could be established. He had been putting pressure on the two powers to secure that goal.

When, in May, 1905, the Japanese approached him to serve as mediator, he agreed. The negotiations carried on at Portsmouth, New Hampshire, were extremely delicate. It was easy to settle minor points, but both nations regarded one issue as crucial; Japan demanded that Russia pay her a cash indemnity and that she be given the island of Sakhalin. The Russians refused to pay the Japanese one cent, and several times threatened to walk out of the conference. Roosevelt would then bend every effort to smooth down ruffled feelings, and keep the conference going.

For days the arguments went on, with neither side budging an inch. Finally, on August 28th, the Japanese agreed to a compromise suggested by Roosevelt; Russia would not pay a cash indemnity, but would give Japan the southern half of Sakhalin Island. The bargain was struck, and the war was brought to an end.

The importance of Roosevelt's mediation can be assessed fairly easily. From a humanitarian point of view, the cessation of hostilities saved thousands of lives. From an international point of view, he helped establish a balance of power in the Pacific. Also, as a result of the reputation he won as a mediator, in 1906, he helped to settle a dispute between France and Germany, which otherwise could have plunged Europe into war.

Roosevelt was awarded the Nobel Prize in 1906 for his successful efforts at Portsmouth. He turned over the money to a board of trustees as an endowment for industrial peace. He considered the development of industrial peace more essential than international peace and thought "it fitting and appropriate to devote the Peace Prize to such a purpose."

His duties as President prevented him from going to Norway to receive the Prize. But in 1910, on his way home from a hunting trip in Africa, he visited Norway and presented his Nobel address.

Urged by his friends, he decided to seek office again in 1912, and since William Howard Taft had control of the regular Republican organization, Roosevelt was forced to campaign on the platform of a separatist movement, the Progressive or Bull Moose party. This split the Republicans and the Democratic candidate, Woodrow Wilson, won the election.

Roosevelt settled down to write his memoirs, but his restless energy drove him to explore the jungles of the Amazon, where he contracted a fever. He was first taken ill in February, 1918. At four o'clock on the morning of January 6, 1919, he died in his home at Oyster Bay, New York, as a result of a blood clot in the coronary artery.

Ernesto Teodoro Moneta
Italy's Great Agitator for Peace

1833–1918

ERNESTO TEODORO MONETA, a most unlikely winner of the Nobel Prize for Peace, was born on September 20, 1833. The son of an ardent Italian patriot who dreamed of a united Italy, as a child Ernesto was exposed to the slogans, passwords and secret organizations that formed part of the revolutionary underground in his native city of Milan. The Austrians had for years ruled the ancient city as they ruled most of northern Italy, and the tide of revolution was running strong. People were tired of strange rulers; they wanted freedom and were prepared to pay almost any price to get it. In the years of Moneta's youth, there were uprisings throughout Italy: in Savoy, in Piedmont, in Modena, in Sicily and, in 1848, in Milan.

When the Milanese manned the barricades thrown across the narrow streets of the city for five days, Moneta, with his father and brothers, took part in the fighting. Largely without plans, without organization and without good leadership, but outnumbering the Austrians and motivated by a determination to succeed, the Milanese drove the enemy out of the city.

In terms of the brave Italian and Austrian men who died, the various uprisings in Italy proved to be tragic fiascos. The Austrians were too strong for the disorganized bands of patriots to break their hold on the country. What the revolutionaries needed, and what they were eventually to find in France, was a powerful nation to come to their aid. Only then could Italy be unified. Meantime, the fighting went on and Moneta was deeply involved.

When a youth undertakes to play a man's role in revolution, he must pay the same penalties that a man must pay if the revolution fails. In Moneta's case, the penalty was exile. He fled to Piedmont and entered the military academy of Ivrea. There he received the kind of training that prepared him for revolutionary fighting. Revolt did break out again, and Moneta and his four brothers enlisted under the banner of the patriotic hero, Giuseppe Garibaldi.

His service with Garibaldi, in the next couple of years in Italy, was arduous and dangerous. Moneta survived and rose to become a member of Garibaldi's General Staff, to help in the planning of several battles. Then, France entered the war in 1859 and the Kingdom of Italy was proclaimed in 1861.

After his discharge, Moneta entered the field of journalism. Within one year he became the editor of a newspaper. Under his direction *Il Secolo* became the most widely read newspaper in Italy. As a member of the international peace movement after 1870, Moneta used the pages of his newspaper to promote the concept of international amity and he is credited with almost single-handedly solidifying friendly relations between France and Italy.

If Moneta had done no more than help heal Italo-French relations, it would have been a significant contribution to peace. But, in 1878, he organized a peace conference in Milan; ten years later, he established the first and the strongest of the Italian peace organizations, known as the Lombard Union. Then, Moneta promoted a convention in Milan which brought together French and Italian Deputies in a successful effort to establish good relations between the two countries. In 1895, having grown famous as Italy's "apostle of peace," he proposed to the delegates attending a session of the World Peace Congress at Antwerp an "appeal to the nations" for peace—an idea accepted by that congress.

In 1896, after thirty years of fruitful association with *Il Secolo*, Moneta retired. He had been one of the greatest editors in Italian newspaper history. Not only had he built up the widest circulation of any paper in that country, he had also proven to be a man of principle. For thirty years he fought for peace and international solidarity; hardly an issue of *Il Secolo* came off press without an article devoted to that theme, or one attacking Francophobia or those who promoted hatred of Austria. Aware that standing armies are a constant threat to peace, he fought to have Italy's army transformed into a citizen militia and, although he failed, his articles helped to furnish ammunition for Italy's men of peace.

A man of great energy, Moneta could not rest and, two years after terminating his association with *Il Secolo,* he founded *La Vita Internazionale.* Again, he took up the cudgels for peace and for friendly relations between nations. How well he succeeded is indicated by the fact that in 1903, when an arbitration treaty was signed between France and Italy, Moneta was hailed as the man most responsible for creating the climate in which such a treaty could be signed.

It was a great tribute, but a greater one was yet to come. After serving as president of the Fifteenth International Peace Congress at Milan in 1906, Moneta was informed, in late 1907, that he was to share the Nobel Peace Prize with Louis Renault of France.

Moneta, undoubtedly, deserved the Prize, but it should be

kept in mind that it was awarded in 1907, when Moneta's record was unblemished.

Four years later, he supported the Italian occupation of Libya which was blatant imperialism and hardly conducive to international peace. Three years later when World War I broke out, Moneta backed Italy's entry into the war on the side of the Allies, largely because they offered her the most!

After his death in 1918 in Milan, the question was often asked if Moneta *was* a man of peace? The answer must be both yes and no. As a youth, he embraced war as a means of achieving national unification. As a man, unification achieved, he worked indefatigably to promote peace, not only because he was convinced that peace would benefit nations internationally but also because Italy desperately needed peace. Finally, as an old man, convinced that Italy, too, must insure her place in the sun if she were to survive, he embraced war again. It is possible that Moneta was more of a patriot than a citizen of the world, but it cannot be denied that, regardless of motivation, Moneta did make a solid contribution to international peace.

Louis Renault
Peace Through International Law

1843–1918

LOUIS RENAULT, who shared the Prize with Moneta in 1907, was one of a quartet of international lawyers dominating the various peace conferences and congresses at the turn of the twentieth century. Considered to be the most important of the jurisprudents, always referred to with respect and admiration, his reputation became international in scope in the last years of his life.

He was born into a respectable, upper middle-class family in Autun, France, on May 21, 1843. Determined from an early age to be a lawyer, after successfully completing his studies at the local lycée, he entered the Paris Law School in 1861. Blessed with a logical and imaginative mind, he did exceptionally well and was graduated with highest honors.

But Renault spent little time practicing his profession. He took his bar exams in 1868 and was admitted to practice. However, when offered a position as professor of law at the University of Dijon, he accepted.

It was the beginning of a great teaching career. From 1868 to 1875 at Dijon and then, until the end of his life in 1918, at the University of Paris, Renault gained a reputation as the most gifted professor of law in Europe. Hundreds of bright young men flocked to Paris to study international law under him. As one writer put it, he brought to the teaching of law "the conceptions of the philosopher, the experience of the historian, and the training of the jurist."

Renault was more than just a great teacher. In 1875, he was one of the founding members of the Institute of International Law. In 1880, he became Director of the French Diplomatic Archives. In the following decade, he published a vast number of articles dealing with various aspects of the law of nations and, in 1889, the first of a seven-volume study, *Traits de droit commercial.* A new career opened in 1890, when he was appointed Jurisconsult of the Ministry of Foreign Affairs.

As jurisconsult, Renault filled a variety of roles of which two were of primary importance. First, he was *the* authority on international law for the Republic of France, the man responsible for French foreign policy insofar as it depended upon the law of nations. Secondly, it was he who represented France at a score of international conferences ranging from the one at The Hague in 1893 to the London Naval Conference of 1908.

Renault's presence at the conferences was very important, not only because of his knowledge of international law, but because his legal understanding, his passionate honesty, his dedication to accomplishing the tasks at hand and a magnetic personality made him a leader in any gathering. Insisting that the groups with which he was associated concern themselves with specifics, he was largely responsible for the achievements of the conferences held at The Hague to discuss private international law; and, to a lesser degree, for the achievements of the peace conference held there in 1899. He also made an important contribution to the revised Red Cross Convention of 1906 which extended the Geneva Accord of 1864 to include naval warfare.

Obviously, Renault was an extraordinary man, evidenced by the fact that, appointed to a position on the Permanent Court of Arbitration—established at The Hague in 1899—his reputation for impartiality was such that nations began to request his services as a judge even in disputes involving France! He was utterly trustworthy, no matter what nation was involved.

Tall, well-built, with finely molded features and a deep, infectious laugh, Renault was the incarnation of benevolence and good will. Utterly modest, he hadn't the slightest idea that he had been proposed for the Peace Prize. But the telegram informing him that he had won arrived on December 10, 1907, and a few months later he made his acceptance speech. His talk centered upon the crucial issue of justice, and how it must serve as a base if there is to be peace between nations.

The winning of this great honor could not be the culmination of a career, only an event in Renault's busy life. He continued his work on the Court of Arbitration and continued publishing and teaching. War came when he was seventy-one and, like so many men, he had to stand by and watch years of work crumble in the dust.

On February 7, 1918, he delivered his last lecture. That evening the greatest teacher of his generation died unexpectedly in his home in Barbizon, Seine-et-Marne.

Klas Pontus Arnoldson

A Prophet Without Honor

1844–1916

Of the various winners of the Nobel Prize for Peace, none reflects better than Klas Pontus Arnoldson the maxim found in the thirteenth chapter of St. Matthew, "A prophet is not without honor, save in his own country." When Arnoldson received the Prize in 1908, there was criticism of the award as an insult to Sweden and as an outrage. It was even suggested that he had come seriously close to being a traitor when, in the dispute leading to the dissolution of the union between Norway and Sweden in 1905, he considered the arguments of Norway the most valid and did everything in his power to promote a peaceful separation.

The man destined to arouse so much criticism was born on October 27, 1844, in Göteborg, a large port city located on the Kattegat in southwestern Sweden. After completing his secondary schooling, Arnoldson found a position as a clerk in a railway office, and settled down to what might have been a humdrum existence had he not involved himself in peace work.

What particularly revolted Arnoldson about war, and made him a confirmed pacifist by the 1860's, was not only the horror of war, but the stupidity of people who allowed themselves to be used by so-called statesmen whose goals were to achieve national ends by means of war. The struggle of Denmark in 1864 against Austria and Prussia as well as the Franco-Prussian War in 1870 were both cases in point. Both were caused by the machinations of Otto von Bismarck, resulting in the unification of Germany. But Arnoldson wondered whether unification was worth the collective agony of the men who were killed or wounded.

He thought not. But what could he do? As an obscure railway stationmaster, he could hardly command much of an audience for his views. If he were going to be listened to, he needed a platform. So, in 1880, he put aside his career as a railroad man to devote himself to journalism and politics.

For a man with no training in either field, he did surprisingly well. His articles on peace in magazines and newspapers were read with great attention, and he proved so influential as a speaker that, in 1882, he was elected to the lower chamber of the Riksdag (the Swedish parliament).

In the years that followed, Arnoldson made effective use of this position. In 1883, he was instrumental in founding the Swedish Peace and Arbitration Union and, in that same year, he submitted to Parliament an address to the King expressing the view that the Government ought to announce the permanent neutrality of Sweden. Parliament refused to accept the address, but did declare that the Government ought to work in that direction. In 1885, he attempted to form a Scandinavian peace organization, but the time was not right for such a group and he failed.

The burden of normal legislative work, coupled with his failure to form the peace organization, led Arnoldson to believe he could be more effective if he removed himself from politics and became a lecturer and writer for peace on a full-time basis. In 1887, he refused to run for office and freed himself from parliamentary concerns.

Arnoldson was convinced that war could be averted only if nations were prepared to arbitrate their disputes. But governments, used to settling international disputes by war, would not adopt the principle of arbitration unless urged to do so by the people they represented. One of the major tasks of the peace workers was to convince the citizens of various countries that arbitration was the only road to peace. To that end, Arnoldson devoted the remainder of his life.

During 1889 and the early part of 1890, he embarked upon an extensive lecture tour through Sweden and Norway. In town after town, he pleaded the cause of arbitration and the peaceful settling of disputes, with special emphasis on the problem of dissolving the Norwegian-Swedish Union peacefully. After one of his lectures in Skien, a local representative of the Storting engaged him in conversation, and agreed that the principle of arbitration ought to be adopted by the legislature. A few months later, in 1890, as a result of an address by that representative, the Storting became the first national assembly to go on record in favor of settling international disputes by arbitration. Indirectly, Arnoldson was the "father" of this historic act.

Although constantly involved in lecturing, not only on peace but on such topics as religious liberty and equality for women, Arnoldson published extensively—essays, articles, stories, a pacifist novel and a number of pamphlets dealing with the forthcoming division between Norway and Sweden. In a sense, this event was a test case for the principle of the peaceful settling of disputes.

In 1815, the Norwegian Storting had declared Norway a Kingdom united with Sweden under one King. But as the decades passed, the Norwegians wanted their own King, and the question arose whether Sweden would allow Norway to go her way in peace. Norway favored arbitration. Sweden had to be convinced.

Perhaps there was no real possibility of war, for the bulk of the Swedes wanted peace. However, Arnoldson and others like him could not be sure, so they wrote and lectured about the subject constantly. In 1905, their efforts were rewarded. The Norwegian Storting declared the Union dissolved, and the Swedish Riksdag acquiesced. There was no war. But a large group in Sweden, who did not want the Union dissolved, was outraged. In 1908, when Arnoldson was awarded the Peace Prize, with Frederik Bajer of Denmark, articles of protest appeared in some newspapers and magazines. Arnoldson was not particularly concerned by the protests.

The Nobel laureate, although poor by most standards, did not use the money for personal needs. He donated it to the various peace organizations with which he was associated.

The last eight years of his life were spent in active pursuit of peace. He died on February 20, 1916, in Stockholm, Sweden.

Frederik Bajer
Soldier Turned Pacifist

1839–1922

FREDERIK BAJER was born on April 21, 1839, in Vestergede, Denmark, the son of an obscure clergyman.

His father was determined that Frederik would have a good education and, at eleven, he was sent to Sorö Academy, the best Danish boarding school at that time.

Frederik became absorbed in history, and was captivated by some of the great figures he studied. He was particularly impressed by Napoleon and, in his schoolboy fancies, he became Napoleon, even going so far as to practice the writing of proclamations to imaginary soldiers in the Napoleonic manner.

Either to escape an education that did not satisfy him or because he aspired to become a great military leader, Bajer decided to become a soldier. In the autumn of 1854, he enrolled in the National Cadet Academy at Copenhagen, and two years later he was appointed a lieutenant of cavalry.

Peacetime army life can be deadly boring for anyone with an active mind. Having such a mind, Bajer took advantage of his leisure to broaden his knowledge. Interested in social and humanitarian problems, he read extensively and published several articles on educational matters. Then, in 1864, the peace of Europe was destroyed by the onslaught of war.

The war pitted Denmark against Prussia and Austria over the duchies of Schleswig and Holstein. The Danes fought heroically, but were overwhelmed by superior forces. The victors took Schleswig and Holstein, and, through no fault of his, Frederik Bajer found himself without a profession. During the conflict he had performed honorably under the most difficult circumstances and had been promoted to the rank of first lieutenant. But, with the war over, the Government decided to reduce the size of the Army, and Bajer was among the officers discharged. Actually, he had grown sick of military service. A schoolboy's dreams were one thing, the reality of military life quite another. The dead and broken bodies he had seen on the battlefield were a tragic substitute for the conference table. Bajer had also become an opponent of war and was determined to begin what he called his "peace service."

When he laid aside his uniform, Bajer was faced with the problem of having to support himself. It was fortunate that he had not wasted his leisure time while in service, but had become proficient in French and the Scandinavian languages and had read widely in history. He decided to become a teacher. His salary was small, but he supplemented his income by serving as a legal translator and as a publicist.

In 1867, Bajer read and was aroused by Frédéric Passy's article describing the founding of the Ligue Internationale et Permanente de la Paix. He attempted to establish a peace society in Denmark, but the moment was inopportune. Having just been defeated in war, the Danes were in no mood for peace societies. In 1870, convinced that hereditary monarchy was a thing of the past and that friendly relations between the Scandinavian countries depended upon their becoming republics, Bajer founded the Association of Scandinavian Free States. In 1871, with his wife, he founded the Danish Woman's Association, which had as its goal the complete equality of women. He delivered lectures, wrote treatises, worked tirelessly in the cause of popular enlightenment, and, in 1872, he was elected to the Danish parliament.

In addition to his formal work as a legislator, Bajer's election gave him a forum in which to advance his ideas. He seized the opportunity to such good effect that, in 1882, he was able to found the Association for the Neutralization of Denmark which, three years later, became the Danish Peace Society.

Naturally, a man so devoted to peace would be interested in bringing together members of the parliaments of Europe to discuss mutual problems. In 1889, at the instigation of Cremer and Passy, invitations were extended to hold the first meeting in Paris. Through Bajer, the Danish Rigsdag was invited to participate. But the proposal was greeted with scorn, and Bajer was the only Danish representative at the founding of the Inter-Parliamentary Union. When the second conference of the IPU was held in London, in 1890, he managed to convince a lone colleague to accompany him. On their return home, they set about forming a Danish inter-parliamentary group. Bajer undertook to interview every member of parliament. He explained, he raged, he cajoled and he succeeded. On February 1st, 1891, such a group was formed, with Bajer as president. In recognition of his services, in 1893, he was elected a member of the Council of the Inter-Parliamentary Union to represent the three Scandinavian countries.

As important as his work in founding the IPU in Denmark was his role in establishing the International Peace Bureau. From the beginning of his involvement in international peace movements, it was clear to Bajer that there must be a central bureau to coordinate peace activities. At the Peace Congress in Rome, in 1891, he succeeded in carrying through the proposal for such a bureau and obtaining the appointment of a provisional committee. Élie Ducommun was appointed director and Bajer became the first chairman of the supervisory committee—a position he retained until 1907.

In 1908, Frederik Bajer was awarded the Nobel Prize for Peace, which he richly deserved. For almost forty-five years he had worked to further the cause of peace, and he had accomplished a great deal. In addition to his other achievements, he had laid the groundwork for the arbitration treaties between Denmark, Holland, Italy and Portugal; he had published several books and many articles dealing with the establishment of permanent peace; and, he was ultimately largely responsible for the fact that, when war broke out in 1914, the Danish people strongly supported unconditional neutrality. Scandinavian neutrality owes much to the work of Frederik Bajer.

After receipt of the Prize, Bajer continued his work. For a time, he hoped that his efforts and those of all the peace workers would be rewarded. There appeared to be a spirit of cooperation developing among the European nations. Tragically, the spirit was more apparent than real. Unable to resolve their problems reasonably, the statesmen of Europe abdicated in favor of war.

World War I was shattering to the hopes of Bajer, but it did not shake his faith in the cause. Expressing his view in the remark, "There is now more need for work in the cause of peace than ever before," he spent the war years, in spite of being painfully ill, attempting to hold together the international groups he had helped create and in laying plans for the future. When peace came again and the Covenant of the League of Nations adopted the principles of law and peace as the basis for international cooperation, Bajer was overjoyed. He saw renewed encouragement for the idea of "peace and justice," the motto of his life's work.

The great expectations of Bajer were not to be realized, and he died on January 22, 1922, still hopeful for the cause he knew to be right.

Auguste Marie François Beernaert
Leader at The Hague Conventions

1829–1912

AUGUSTE MARIE FRANÇOIS BEERNAERT, thirteenth winner of the Nobel Prize for Peace, was born at Ostend on July 26, 1829, a year before Belgium won her struggle for independence.

After his birth, Auguste's father, a civil servant in the revenue department, was assigned to the town of Namur, a small, provincial community. Monsieur Beernaert soon became one of the town's leading citizens, his salary affording his family a good house, servants, a carriage and a private pew in the village church.

The public schools were very poor in the first half of the nineteenth century. For bright students such as young Auguste, these schools were dead ends. Fortunately, his parents mapped out a course of study for him in modern and classical languages, as well as history and mathematics to prepare him for university life. When unable to instruct him personally, they hired tutors.

Their endeavor was a success. For Auguste the pursuit of knowledge early became, and remained, a thing of pleasure. He gained admittance to the University of Louvain and established an outstanding record as a law student.

After graduation he settled in Brussels, passed the bar examination and was admitted to practice.

By all accounts, he was an extremely able lawyer and an impressive figure in the courtroom. Solidly, almost massively built, with black, piercing eyes, his face framed in short whiskers, he usually wore a black frock coat and a high, stiff collar. Possessing an orderly, logical mind and marshaling his arguments with lucid eloquence, he overwhelmed his opponents. Yet out of the courtroom, his manners and actions belied his appearance. In the intimacy of his home, he was courteous, helpful and sociable; very much a gentleman with wide-ranging interests.

It is not certain whether Beernaert's life was carefully planned or if it was sheer coincidence that, exactly twenty years after he became a lawyer and accumulated enough money to insure economic security, he entered politics. In 1873, when Jules Malou, leader of the Catholic party and Prime Minister of Belgium, offered him the office of Minister of Public Works, he accepted without hesitation.

In the parliamentary system, government ministers play a dual role; they are both ministers and members of Parliament, and as the latter they are subject to approval or rejection by the people. When accepting the portfolio of Public Works, Beernaert had to find a constituency that would elect him. After one failure, he ran and was elected in the district of Thielt, in 1874. Moreover, the district was to return him to Parliament without a break until his death.

The government office of Public Works that Beernaert headed included industrial relations, the administration of railways and the merchant marine. Beernaert quickly won the admiration of his colleagues for the efficiency with which his office was administered. In the Chamber of Deputies, he proved to be an asset to the Government in its debates with the Opposition. He had the eloquence of a man intent upon convincing by logic rather than moving by emotion, and within a short time after taking office, he was regarded as one of the outstanding figures in Government.

Between 1878 and 1884, he was part of the Opposition, then he briefly held his old ministerial position when Malou again became Prime Minister. Malou soon quarreled with the King, Leopold II, and resigned. Auguste Beernaert, approved both by his party and the King, succeeded him as Prime Minister.

Even a brief sketch of Beernaert's career as Prime Minister would be hard to follow without some knowledge of the history of Belgium. But he *was* one of the greatest Prime Ministers Belgium ever had and for ten years he governed his country well.

With his resignation in 1894, his effectiveness in internal affairs came to an end. Not that he didn't retain a voice in Government; he was appointed a Minister of State (an honorary title for leading statesmen); he was elected chairman of the assembly and he remained a Deputy until his death.

In his last years as Prime Minister, he had grown increasingly concerned with international problems, and when his tenure in office came to an end, he was free to join with other internationalminded men in a search for solutions.

Given Beernaert's career as lawyer and politician, it is understandable that his efforts in the cause of world peace would be pursued within the framework of a political organization, the Inter-Parliamentary Union.

When the IPU held one of its early meetings in Brussels, in 1893, Beerneart was Prime Minister, and his position prevented him from taking an active part. But he followed the proceedings closely and, whenever possible, lent the weight of his office to further the work being done. However, it was not until 1896 that he finally attended a plenary meeting of the union. From then on, he was one of its more active and more important members. He presided over three conferences in Brussels in 1897, 1905 and 1910. When the Inter-Parliamentary Council was created in 1899, his reputation was such that he was appointed president, and in that capacity, he directed the work of the IPU executive committee and the bureau until his death.

The two major issues engrossing Beernaert's attention in these years were compulsory arbitration and disarmament. He was convinced that if all disputes had to be submitted to an international court of arbitration, and if each state had to abide by the decisions handed down, there would be no wars. The crucial problem was to persuade states to accept the principle of arbitration.

Since, in 1900, most states prided themselves on being "peace loving," the job of Beernaert and others should have been simple. Beernaert truly believed that the goals he set for himself could be attained. He believed that basically men could be reached by rational arguments. So at conference after conference of the IPU, he pleaded his cause, hoping through the membership to reach and sway the governments they represented.

It should be added that Beernaert was actively involved in the codification of international law which, often unclear, had been the cause (and still is) of numerous disputes between nations.

In the area of disarmament he had no success at all. The citizens of the world, he pointed out, were staggering under the burden of the cost of weapons that could only be used for warfare. But the statesmen of Europe were not prepared or willing to listen.

In 1909, for his unceasing efforts to advance the principles of arbitration and disarmament to insure the peace of the world, Auguste Beernaert was awarded the Nobel Prize for Peace, in conjunction with his friend and colleague, d'Estournelles de Constant.

When he received the Prize, Beernaert was eighty years old. He had had a long and honorable career, and he might well have retired and spent the remainder of his life at ease. But he continued to take an active interest in public affairs, particularly in disarmament. At the IPU Conference in Geneva in 1912, he presented a report on the prohibition of air warfare and led his last, successful fight to have the report adopted by the conference.

He died in Lucerne on October 6, 1912.

Baron d'Estournelles de Constant de Rebecque
Peace Through Diplomacy and Conventions

1852–1924

Given their traditional cosmopolitanism, it is remarkable that so few aristocrats have ever been involved in the peace movement. Unfortunately, they have more often than not regarded the peace movement as the province of cranks. Baron d'Estournelles de Constant was one exception.

D'Estournelles was born on November 22, 1852, in the Chateau of Clermont-Creans, in the Loire region of France.

The young baron was an excellent student and, after being graduated with an advanced degree from the School of Oriental Languages in Paris, he traveled in the Orient, then entered the

French Foreign Service in 1876. After a period of training in Paris, d'Estournelles was sent to London, then Tunis, to The Hague, then back to London as counsellor to the French ambassador. By 1890, d'Estournelles stood on the threshold of a brilliant future in the world of diplomacy. It appeared only a matter of time before he was appointed to the highest of all diplomatic positions, ambassador. However, the London assignment was to be his last in the Foreign Service, and for a very good reason. He became a politician.

During the years he had spent in the Foreign Service, d'Estournelles became convinced that diplomacy was not the road to peace, but could come only by the substitution of law for war, which was more the task of the legislator than of a diplomat. So he requested a leave of absence and managed to be elected to the Chamber of Deputies, in 1895.

Small, not quite five-and-a-half feet tall, but possessing a commanding personality, eloquent in debate, and utterly convinced of the justice of his cause, within a few years d'Estournelles became one of the most influential men in the Chamber of Deputies. In 1899, when a conference was held at The Hague to discuss peace, he was, with Léon Bourgeois, the obvious choice of his government to represent France.

The First Hague Conference did not accomplish much. Twenty-six nations met to work out a formula for reducing armaments. But, because of suspicions and jealousies, it proved impossible for them to agree on any general limitation of arms, although some achievements were recorded. An agreement was worked out to restrict the use of certain weapons in war; it was agreed to codify international law with regard to war and, finally, an international court of arbitration was established at The Hague to which nations might submit their quarrels.

Even if the accomplishments were minimal, the conference at least appeared to demonstrate that the nations were interested in talking about peace and that, by agreeing to a court of arbitration, they might eventually accept arbitration in place of war. D'Estournelles, enthusiastic about the meeting and hopeful that it betokened the dawn of a new day, set himself to propagandize the people of Europe and, through them, to force their governments to arbitrate. D'Estournelles had been busy even before the conference. Aware that the public was poorly informed as to the meaning and purpose of the conference, in the months before it met, he delivered explanatory lectures in various cities in France. After the conference, he lectured in Vienna, Scandinavia, England, Italy and in France.

Besides his lectures, d'Estournelles joined with others in successfully persuading President Theodore Roosevelt to submit a Mexican-American dispute to the Court of Arbitration in 1902. D'Estournelles thought that if an important nation like the United States was prepared to arbitrate, then arbitration would grow increasingly important as nations got used to the idea and, eventually, disputes would be arbitrated, ending all wars. Unfortunately, nations preferred waging war to arbitration on all save minor matters.

Lecturing constituted a small portion of d'Estournelles' efforts to help bring about a peaceful world. In 1903, he founded a parliamentary group for international arbitration within the French Government. In order to popularize the idea of voluntary arbitration between France and England, he led the group on a visit to the British Parliament. Since few such visits had ever been exchanged, the visit immediately became famous. In the fall of the same year, British legislators returned the visit and were royally entertained by the French. Convinced that he had found one way to cement international friendship, d'Estournelles, after winning election to the French Senate, arranged for a series of visits from parliament members of Denmark, Norway and Sweden in 1904. These visits were returned by the French in 1909.

In 1905, d'Estournelles founded the Ligue de la Conciliation Internationale, and a periodical, *International Conciliation,* to explain its purpose. Like so many pacifist magazines, *International Conciliation* could command little revenue either from circulation or from advertising. On the verge of failure, it was taken over by the Carnegie Endowment for International Peace. Through his friendship with Nicholas Murray Butler (Laureate in 1931), a friend of Andrew Carnegie, d'Estournelles became the head of the endowment organization in Europe; and Butler became president of the American branch of the *ligue.*

In 1909, for his unceasing effort to further the cause of arbitration and conciliation, and hence world peace, d'Estournelles was awarded, with August Beernaert of Belgium, the Nobel Prize for Peace.

In the few years remaining before the outbreak of war, d'Estournelles served on the executive committee of the Inter-Parliamentary Union, lectured and published extensively on topics associated with peace.

During the war years, there could be no question of conciliation or arbitration. For four long and bitter years, the conflict raged. Finally, in 1918, it came to an end.

With the ending of hostilities, organizations devoted to peace once again took heart. When the Inter-Parliamentary Union met again in Stockholm in 1921, d'Estournelles tried to create an atmosphere in which peace could flourish.

However, during World War I hatred had so deeply penetrated the hearts of Germans and Frenchmen that the French branch of the IPU refused to associate with the German branch. In spite of all his efforts, d'Estournelles failed to bring about a reconciliation.

As diplomat, Deputy, and Senator of France, d'Estournelles had been involved in public affairs for forty-five years and had done a great deal to help establish peace. But what he witnessed at the Stockholm conference was heartbreaking. He began a slow withdrawal from public life and, on May 15, 1924, he died in Bordeaux, France.

Tobias Michael Carel Asser
International Lawyer and Jurist

1838–1913

On April 29, 1838, four years before the publication of Tennyson's prophetic poem, "Locksley Hall," Tobias Michael Carel Asser was born in Amsterdam, Holland. In his poem, as though sketching the career of the future Nobel Prize winner, the poet conjured up for the reader a vision of a world federation; the war drums stilled, peace would come, and "the kindly earth shall slumber, lapt in universal law." Asser was not a world federalist; he was an international lawyer, one who believed that fundamentally peace is dependent upon law binding not only upon nations but upon the individuals who make the nations what they are.

Asser's early years are obscure, but, since he attended the university in his native city, it can be assumed that the family possessed at least a modest amount of money. He must have been a brilliant student, as he graduated from the university and was appointed professor of commercial law by the time he was twenty-four.

Once established as a professor of law, Asser's reputation, based upon teaching and publishing, grew with giant strides. Aware of the dearth of publications in the field of international law, in 1869 he joined with two other nationally known lawyers in founding *The Review of International Law and Comparative Legislation.* The *Review* proved successful because it was one of the first in the field of international law, and because of the quality of material in the publication. Asser took the lead in founding, in 1873, what was to become one of the most important legal bodies in Western Europe, the Institute of International Law (which won the Nobel Peace Prize in 1904).

The same year that he brought the institute into being, he was called by the Government to become legal adviser to the Minister of Foreign Affairs for the Netherlands. This position still allowed him to lecture at the university and to continue writing. Between 1875 and 1893, besides producing many articles, he published three volumes on international law that were rapidly accepted as outstanding works of their kind.

Asser was a popular lecturer at the University of Amsterdam, and he enjoyed his work. But, after thirty-one years of teaching, he retired. His work as legal adviser to the Foreign Minister, his great reputation as a legal authority, author and teacher, combined to make him the logical choice when a vacancy occurred on the State Council in 1893. He accepted the appointment and moved into a position where he was able to influence government policy.

Convinced, as were many other international lawyers of that day, that peace could be achieved through legalistic means, Asser was instrumental as a member of the State Council in persuading the Government to call a conference on international law at The Hague late in 1893. He was the presiding officer; beautifully organized, precise, methodical and a master of oratory, he did a splendid job. When, the following year, another conference was held at The Hague, he again occupied the president's chair.

Afterwards, for a number of years, Asser was thoroughly involved in international affairs. In 1899, he was the Netherlands' chief delegate to The Hague Peace Conference on international law and, when the Permanent Court of Arbitration was established at The Hague, he was appointed a member. In 1902, he acted as an arbiter in a dispute between the United States and Mexico— one of the first disputes to be submitted to the court for arbitration —and a year later he was again elected the presiding officer at The Hague Conference.

Such an enviable record could not fail to influence the decisions of his own government when state offices fell vacant. In 1904, he was made Dutch Minister of State, the highest position someone not of royal blood could attain.

Occupied with affairs of state, and busy on the Court of Arbitration, Asser found time to attend one more international meeting. In 1907, a Second Hague Peace Conference was held and Asser served as chief delegate from the Netherlands. The conference accomplished little. Nations were not ready or willing to unite in search of peace.

The Nobel Committee, reflecting the then common belief of most peace workers that only law could give substance to their efforts, divided the Peace Prize of 1911 between Tobias Asser and Alfred Fried of Austria. While, technically, only two of the conferences with which Asser was associated were "peace" conferences, the rest were certainly called to establish the kind of foundation upon which the structure of peace could be erected.

Asser died on July 29, 1913, in The Hague.

Alfred Hermann Fried
Publicist and Propagandist for Peace

1864–1921

It is a tragic commentary on the cause of peace that many men who were famous in the peace movement in Western Europe after 1860 have passed into oblivion. Not only is this true of leaders like Hodgson Pratt, the great English pacifist, but Nobel Laureates of Peace have also been forgotten, unless they happened to have made their reputations in other fields. The origins and life of a once-important man could hardly be more obscure than those of Alfred Hermann Fried.

Little is known of his birth and youth beyond the fact that he was born in Vienna on November 11, 1864, and that he was trained as a bookseller. He is supposed to have become a peace advocate as a result of viewing some antiwar canvases done by a Russian painter. It is also believed that Fried felt he was completely alone in his opposition to war until, quite by accident, he happened to read an article about the founding of the Austrian Peace Society by Bertha von Suttner. The article aroused his enthusiasm and he immediately dashed off a note to the baroness proposing that she edit a new peace journal which he would found. This was Fried's formal introduction into the peace movement.

The Baroness von Suttner was impressed with Fried's note, and she agreed to Fried's suggestion that they establish a journal. Since her name was famous, she also agreed to edit it, and, in 1892, the magazine *Die Waffen Nieder* came into being. Carrying the same title as Bertha von Suttner's novel, it immediately attracted the attention of the European public interested in the cause of peace.

Almost single-handedly, Fried founded the German Peace Society in 1892 and, between 1894 and 1899, he published, besides *Die Waffen Nieder,* the *Monatliche Friedenskorrespondenz (Monthly Peace Correspondent).*

In 1899, after spending several years in Germany where he devoted himself to the affairs of the Peace Society and its newsletter, Fried moved back to Vienna. When Baroness von Suttner tired of editing *Die Waffen Nieder* in 1899, Fried decided to establish another journal, this one entitled *Die Friedens-Warte.*

In 1911, for his work on *Die Waffen Nieder* and later on *Die Friedens-Warte,* for his founding of the German Peace Society, and for the publication of several books, including *The Problem of Disarmament* and *Pan-America,* Alfred Fried was awarded the Nobel Prize for Peace. He shared the Prize with Tobias Asser; yet if wholehearted dedication, a willingness to subordinate all interests to peace, are among the criteria established for Nobel Prize winners, then Fried was the more deserving of the two.

When war came in 1914, Fried was forced to flee from Austria. His work in the peace movement and biting articles against the Austrian government resulted in Fried being accused of high treason. He found refuge in Switzerland, where he lived in exile during the war.

Returning to Austria after the war, he published the pacifist writings of the Baroness von Suttner under the title *The Struggle to Prevent the World War* and a series of articles in which he bitterly attacked the rulers of Germany for causing the war. But the peace movement had been practically crushed, and peace prophets were still without honor in their own lands. Fried sank into obscurity and he died quietly in Vienna on May 6, 1921.

Elihu Root

Peace in the Western Hemisphere

1845–1937

ELIHU ROOT early developed the will and determination that made him a leader in his profession and a leader of men. Elihu's father's family went back in American history to 1637. His maternal grandfather, with whom he spent much time as a youth, was the son of the man who commanded the Americans at Concord Bridge, in 1775.

Root's father was a professor of mathematics in Hamilton College, near the little town of Clinton, New York, where Elihu was born in 1845. There were some advantages in being the son of a college professor. His father's income was steady, he possessed a fairly good library, had a wide variety of interests and he encouraged his children to develop their minds.

Elihu took advantage of his father's library and he entered Hamilton College when he was fifteen, the youngest in a class of fifty-four. Four years later he was graduated Phi Beta Kappa and class valedictorian.

A college graduate at nineteen, he was faced with the choice of a profession and the need to be self-supporting. In 1865 he arrived in New York City determined to be a lawyer; he applied and was accepted at Columbia Law School and then found a position teaching history in a girls' school. His future was more or less secure, and he settled down to work.

Two years later, in the summer of 1867, he was admitted to the New York Bar, and was hired immediately by one of the city's leading law firms. Root advanced rapidly in his profession. Although involved in some important cases dealing with public interests, the bulk of his practice dealt with railroads, banks, wills and estates—an extremely lucrative practice. By the time he was forty, he was earning as much as a hundred thousand dollars a year.

Root, from his early years in New York, had involved himself in political affairs. He was a friend of Chester A. Arthur who, when he became President, appointed Root as United States Attorney for the southern district of New York. The position paid only six thousand dollars a year, but it afforded Root the time to pursue his own practice, and it gave him opportunity to be of service to the community.

By the mid-1890's, Root had become a power in New York politics. In the forefront of the fight for clean government, he often clashed with the bosses within his own party, and in 1898, he helped Theodore Roosevelt to be elected governor. Having no desire for personal advancement, he was surprised when, in July, 1899, he received a call from the White House asking him to become Secretary of War! Root replied, "Thank the President for me, but say that it is quite absurd, I know nothing about war, I know nothing about the Army." Back came the reply, "President McKinley . . . has got to have a lawyer to direct the Government of these Spanish Islands, and you are the lawyer he wants."

Root had to make up his mind instantly; to decide what "kind of a lawyer I wished to be. . . ." For him, there was only one answer; "so I went to perform a lawyer's duty upon the call of the greatest of all clients, the Government of the United States."

He was strikingly successful. Demonstrating his unbelievable capacity for hard work and working with General Leonard Wood in Cuba and William Howard Taft in the Philippines, he initiated model systems of colonial government. He devised methods whereby the people were immediately involved in self-government, he used the Army to build roads and hospitals, and to develop systems of sanitation, an absolute must for a healthy people in tropical lands.

In spite of the fact that he became ill several times through overwork, Root was happy at the War Department. However, Mrs. Root did not care for the life of a Cabinet member's wife. She much preferred the privacy of her home, and the companionship of her family, so Root resigned from office in February, 1904.

Root could not foresee that he would be absent from Washington only eighteen months. In the summer of 1905, John Hay died, and Theodore Roosevelt appealed to Root to become Secretary of State, an appeal which Root could not resist.

At the turn of the twentieth century, relations between the United States and Latin America were very bad. In 1898 the United States had taken Cuba, physically extending its power into the Caribbean. In 1903 the United States moved into the Dominican Republic. In 1904 it got control of the Canal Zone. In 1904 Theodore Roosevelt announced that misbehavior in Latin America "may force the United States . . . to the exercise of an international power." As a result of all this, Latin America viewed the United States with deep suspicion.

Root believed that if the United States and Latin America embraced the idea of arbitrating their disputes, there would be no need for interference on the part of the United States. With this in mind, he undertook the task of cultivating friendly relations with Latin American diplomats in Washington and, in 1906, he announced that he would attend a conference of American nations in Rio de Janeiro.

Root's trip achieved two important things. At the Rio conference, he agreed to the principle of arbitration, and in every country he visited he preached a new doctrine of sympathy, cooperation and understanding between nations.

When Root retired as Secretary of State in 1909, he had every reason to be proud of his record. He had inaugurated the "good neighbor" policy toward Latin America. He had helped settle a major dispute with England over the Newfoundland fisheries, he had helped to keep the country at peace.

In 1909, Root was sixty-four years old, and he was content to return to his law practice. But the doors of the State Department had no more than closed behind him when the portals of the Senate swung open. On January 19, he was nominated for senator by the New York legislature.

There is a certain irony in the fact that, during the vicious political fight in 1912 between his friends Roosevelt and Taft (a fight in which Root was involved), he should have been awarded the Peace Prize. The Nobel Committee bestowed it upon him for his contributions toward peace in the Western Hemisphere, for his insistence upon the sanctity of treaties and for the work he had done in setting up an enlightened colonial system.

He regarded the award not as a personal tribute, but as a "conservative European approval of the conduct of the American Government in colonial and foreign affairs during the administrations of McKinley and Roosevelt."

When his term as senator was over, Root did not run for re-election. He was over seventy years old and tired of public life. He did allow himself to be boomed for the Presidency in 1916, but was relieved when Hughes won the nomination.

In 1937, at the age of ninety-two, Elihu Root died. He had begun his career in politics as a champion of clean government; he emerged upon the world state as a humanitarian and he won the highest award the world can offer for his effort to promote peace between nations.

Henri Marie La Fontaine

The Last Prewar Peace Worker

1854–1943

HENRI LA FONTAINE was born and died in the midst of war. When he was born in Belgium on April 22, 1854, France and England were blocking Russia's attempt to get control of the strait of the Dardanelles. When he died, in 1943, these powers were united in blocking Hitler's attempt to get control of the world.

La Fontaine attended the University of Brussels and was admitted as an advocate to the Court of Appeals by the time he was twenty-three.

For a man of cascading energy, earning a living before the bar was not enough. He early developed an interest in education, and in 1878 became secretary of a technical school for young women. The position gave him an opportunity to incorporate his ideas into the operation of the school. He was so successful and original that, within a few decades, the technical school became a model for hundreds of other schools in Belgium and in other countries. This experience also enabled him to help found a new university in Brussels in 1893-94. La Fontaine was chosen by his colleagues for the chair of international law (in which he made himself an expert).

The man responsible for interesting La Fontaine in the peace movement was the English pacifist, Hodgson Pratt. In 1883, Pratt visited Belgium to encourage the peace movement there. Not a peace advocate at the time, La Fontaine was impressed by Pratt and became an immediate convert. By 1889, the Belgian Arbitration and Peace Society was founded and La Fontaine became its secretary-general.

Between the years 1880 and 1895, La Fontaine found time to interest himself in politics. Unable to identify with the Catholic-Aristocratic party, in 1891 he became a member of the Socialist party. Four years later, having helped to organize the Sixth International Peace Congress at Antwerp, he became a Socialist member of the Belgian parliament.

As a member of the senate, in the years following and before World War I, La Fontaine held a commanding position in every international peace congress and inter-parliamentary union conference he attended. He was on the special committee of the Peace Congress in 1895 which prepared a plan for a permanent Court of Arbitration. On the death of Frederik Bajer, he was elected president of the Bureau International Permanent de la Paix, a post he held until his death. He organized a Congress of International Associations, set up its central office, edited its publication *La Vie Internationale* and served as a reporter to the Geneva Convention in 1912.

Nor was this all; in conjunction with a friend, he founded and became the director of the International Institute of Bibliography which, in its headquarters in Brussels, served as a clearing house for pacifist literature published anywhere in the world. In 1897, he founded the House of Documentation, a gigantic undertaking, to prove that everything ever said in writing anywhere in the world could be indexed and made available on a moment's notice.

In 1902 La Fontaine published a volume still considered a standard reference work for students. Entitled *The Code of International Arbitration: Documentary History of International Arbitration*, it was an exhaustive study of every arbitration treaty in the Western world, beginning with the one between the United States and England in 1794 and extending up to 1900.

In 1913, with the Western powers on the verge of a war, La Fontaine was awarded the Nobel Prize for Peace. Since the turn of the century, no man had done more for peace and few had done as much.

When World War I came to an end, La Fontaine was sixty-five. While he was still active, the years of almost incredible effort were over. He served his government as a member of the delegation to the Paris Peace Conference and as its delegate to the First League Assembly. As the "grand old man" of the peace movement, he served as president of the IPU's Committee on Juridical Questions and as a member of the IPU Council. He also continued to work in the House of Documentation.

Finally, in 1936, at the age of eighty-two, he retired from his long and honorable career as a Senator. He did not retire from the peace movement. Nothing but death could force that; and death came on May 14, 1943, in the midst of a world torn apart by hatred and war.

Thomas Woodrow Wilson
The League of Nations

1856–1924

THOMAS WOODROW WILSON, born on December 26, 1856, in Staunton, Virginia, was anything but a picture of health. A delicate, acutely sensitive boy, he remained at home until the age of nine, taking advantage of his father's library, and dreaming of the day when he would be Senator Woodrow Wilson from Virginia.

At the age of eighteen, a tall, lanky youth with a thatch of fair hair, wide, searching eyes, a sense of humor and quick intelligence, Wilson journeyed north to attend Princeton University. There he prepared himself for his career which, initially, was to be in education rather than in politics.

He was graduated from Princeton in 1879, forty-first in a class of a hundred and twenty-six. Although he was not a top student, Wilson was capable of producing work of extraordinary maturity. In his senior year, he wrote an article on "Cabinet Government in the United States," which was published in one of the best magazines of that day, the *International Review*.

After graduation, Wilson enrolled in the University of Virginia law school. Following a period of ill health, when he was forced to leave the university, Wilson took the bar examinations in Georgia and started to practice law in Atlanta. Within a year, he turned from law practice to postgraduate work in political science at Johns Hopkins University, and did remarkably well. In his second year, he was awarded one of the two fellowships offered in the department, and by the time he left to accept a teaching position, he had completed *Congressional Government* which, apart from selling well, won him his Ph.D., in 1886.

In 1885, Wilson accepted his first position, as associate professor of history at Bryn Mawr. He worked hard on a book, published a number of articles, and delivered lectures at Johns Hopkins. In 1889, *The State* was published. It was a scholarly achievement, and strengthened his reputation as one of the bright young men in the academic world.

His fame as a lecturer spread and, as a result, in 1902, Woodrow Wilson was chosen to be the new president of Princeton University. As president, Wilson had a few supremely happy years. He initiated several major reforms that helped make the university great. But when he tried to abolish Princeton's eating clubs (they were much like the modern fraternities), he met his first defeat.

He was defeated again in a struggle over the status of the graduate school. This time Wilson clashed with the alumni and the trustees. Something had to give. The trustees decided it would be Wilson, and he was asked to resign in 1910. This terminated his academic career, but paved his way to greatness.

That same year, he accepted an invitation to be the Democratic gubernatorial candidate in New Jersey. The Democratic party was corrupt and riddled with strife. But it was believed the time was propitious for the party to take over the governorship from the Republicans if the right man could be found behind whom the party would unite. The state's political bosses decided that Wilson was such a man, and he agreed to run if no strings were attached.

When the campaign began, much to the professionals' surprise, Wilson proved so effective a campaigner that he was elected by one of the largest majorities in New Jersey history. The bosses were even more surprised when he succeeded, within the first year of his governorship, to make New Jersey almost a model state, attracting attention to himself as a figure of political importance in the United States. His prestige was so great that at the Democratic Convention of 1912, he was nominated for the Presidency of the United States.

In two years he moved from the presidency of Princeton to the Presidency of the United States! Never in American history had a man moved so far so fast.

During Wilson's two administrations, 1913 and 1914 were the most productive years, with a great deal of major legislation enacted by Congress. Then, with his program only half-completed, a catastrophe occurred. The Austrian Archduke Francis Ferdinand was assassinated at Sarajevo, and a few weeks later the flames of World War I engulfed Europe.

During the crucial years of 1915 and 1916, Wilson fought desperately to maintain American neutrality, but in February of 1917, Germany launched a submarine attack upon neutral shipping and Wilson's hand was forced. On April 2, 1917, he faced the assembled Congress of the United States and, asking for a declaration of war against the Central Powers, said the United States would fight for the peace of the world.

Wilson knew there would be no peace in victory. Only by

nations uniting together would peace be assured. And to that end he dedicated America.

The United States involvement was decisive and Germany was beaten. However, the victors were bitter. Germany, the loser, must pay. It was into this maelstrom of emotion that Wilson plunged, when he decided to go to Europe to take part in the peace settlement.

Welcomed with great acclaim on the European continent, he appeared to millions as the savior of the world, the man who would inaugurate a reign of universal peace.

At the conference table, Wilson faced some of the shrewdest politicians in Europe, who knew that Wilson was prepared to sacrifice almost anything to achieve the League of Nations. Playing upon this ideal, they forced Wilson to make concessions. Germany had to assume complete guilt for starting the war, and she had to pay its entire cost. However, written into the peace settlement was the League of Nations. It appeared Wilson had won. The United States was dedicated to peace, and it was unreasonable to think she would refuse to join the League. But that is exactly what happened!

Only the Senate can accept or reject a treaty. There were those in the Senate who hated Wilson and there were others who were isolationists and put up a bitter fight against the League. The Senate set about studying the treaty and several amendments were offered. Had Wilson been prepared to accept the amendments—even those offered just to spite him—the treaty probably would have been ratified. But he refused, and decided to carry the fight to the people. He was warned by his physicians not to do it, but he was determined. The consequences were inevitable. He collapsed after a speech delivered in Pueblo, Colorado. He was rushed back to Washington, partially recovered, then suffered a paralytic stroke.

Crippled in body, the great powers of his mind dimmed by pain and weariness, Wilson could not carry on the fight and the treaty was lost. The United States never joined the League.

Finishing out his term, Wilson lived in Washington until his death on the morning of February 3, 1924.

In 1920, Wilson was honored by a Nobel Prize for Peace. In his acceptance speech, which he could not deliver in person, he said, in part:

> *The cause of peace, and the cause of truth are of one family. Even as those who love science and devote their lives to physics and chemistry, even as those who create new and higher ideals for mankind in literature, even so with those who love peace, there is no limit set. Whatever has been accomplished in the past is petty compared to the glory of the promise of the future.*

Léon Victor Auguste Bourgeois
French Leader for the League

1851–1925

LÉON VICTOR AUGUSTE BOURGEOIS, the twenty-second winner of the Nobel Prize for Peace, was born on May 21, 1851, in Paris, France. The son of a poor watchmaker, he was a brilliant boy and obtained a degree in law in his early twenties.

After passing a series of competitive examinations, Bourgeois won admittance to the civil service where his outstanding ability as an administrator gained immediate recognition. He moved up rapidly, but it was not until he was appointed prefect of police for the Seine Department, in 1887, that he became known to the public. In that year, a scandal forced Jules Grévy to resign from the Presidency of the French Republic and it looked as though

Georges Boulanger might seize power. Partisans and foes of the military hero threatened to use force and violence to gain their own goals. As Prefect of Police, it was Bourgeois' responsibility to stop rioting in the streets before it had a chance to get out of hand. He succeeded, and managed to win the respect of the bulk of the citizens who wanted peace and quiet.

As the man who kept the peace in Paris, Bourgeois became well-known, and he entered a contest with Boulanger in the District of the Marne, in 1888, for a seat in the Chamber of Deputies. Being a product of the working class, Bourgeois' sympathies lay with their hopes and aspirations. He was, politically, a radical. Marne was a working-class district; the workers appreciated Bourgeois' political philosophy, and despite Boulanger's fame, Bourgeois won the election.

In the Chamber of Deputies, he rose with impressive speed. In the same year he became a Deputy, he was named Under Secretary of State for the Interior. In 1890, he became the Minister of Public Instruction; in 1895, he formed his own ministry, also serving as Minister of the Interior. Three years later, he was named the chief French delegate to the First Hague Peace Conference.

Although long convinced of the necessity of arbitration and peace, Bourgeois established his reputation among peace workers with his skillful handling of the Third Commission at The Hague Conference. From the beginning, this commission, charged with the question of international arbitration, was pulled in several directions by delegations intent upon making their own views prevail. Some delegations, such as the German, were adamantly opposed to the whole concept of arbitration. Bourgeois' job as the presiding officer was to enforce compromise, encourage debate, soothe ruffled tempers and exert his authority to keep contesting delegations in line. Not nearly as much came out of the deliberations of the commission as Bourgeois had hoped. He had suggested a plan that would have led to enforced arbitration, but it was rejected. A Permanent Court of Arbitration was provided for, however, and Bourgeois had good reason to hope that, eventually, the nations would adopt a policy of compulsory arbitration.

As the years went by, Bourgeois was elected to the presidency of the Chamber of Deputies, then to the Senate, published a number of books and was appointed to the Permanent Court of Arbitration at The Hague. But by 1913, when he became Premier of France, the nations had begun to rearm. Not even the Second Hague Conference of 1907 had been able to halt the inexorable move toward war. The delegates at that conference, including Bourgeois, fought vigorously for compulsory arbitration. But Germany, and other nations, would have none of it. The conference made some minor gains, but not enough to insure peace. Seven years later, World War I began.

Bourgeois could do little for his cause during the war years. Of course, the men of peace could plan, and in 1917 Bourgeois was appointed chairman of a French commission to study the possibilities for a Society of Nations. A year later, the commission's deliberations were presented by Bourgeois to the peacemakers who gathered in Paris.

His plan was rejected, but Bourgeois labored valiantly to implement the plan for a League of Nations presented by President Wilson. He represented France as a member of the League of Nations Commission at the Peace Conference; and, in 1920, he became the first French Representative to the Council of the League of Nations and was also chosen its first president. That same year he was awarded the Nobel Prize for Peace.

Although he was hailed as the "spiritual father" of the League, the Prize was probably for his long and continuous effort to establish world peace through arbitration. Without Bourgeois' presence at the First Hague Conference, most likely there would have been no Permanent Court of Arbitration. Without that court and its work in laying the groundwork of international cooperation, there could have been no League of Nations.

In the years after 1920, Bourgeois remained associated with the League as the permanent French delegate to Geneva. However, approaching blindness forced him to retire from all but the most pressing tasks. In 1923, he withdrew from his position as president of the French Senate, and on September 29, 1925, he died at the Chateau d'Oger near Épernay.

Karl Hjalmar Branting
Socialist Pacifist for the League

1860–1925

It rarely happens that a member of the upper classes becomes a convinced Socialist, or that such a person becomes a prime minister. Karl Hjalmar Branting became both. Born in 1860, he was sent to one of the most exclusive private schools in Stockholm and, after graduating in 1877, easily gained admission into the University of Upsala. At the university, he majored in mathematics and natural science and dreamed of becoming an astronomer. In 1882 and 1883, he actually served as a secretary at the Astronomical Observatory in Stockholm.

But he turned his back upon the bourgeois world that afforded him ease and security, and became a radical, a socialist and a politician. This remarkable shift occurred at the university, when he became interested in social problems; problems having to do with unemployment, with sickness and health, with security in old age and a decent standard of living for all the people of Sweden. To the young student the political parties were not facing up to the realities of Swedish life, and could not develop answers for the existing problems, much less for problems that were arising as by-products of modernization.

Branting gave up the idea of becoming an astronomer or teacher and, in 1884, he became the editor of a radical newspaper, called *Tiden*, founded by K. P. Arnoldson. However, the paper was forced off the market in 1886 and Branting found himself without a job.

In the two years he had been an editor, Branting's political philosophy had changed drastically. As a result of several trips abroad and meetings with outstanding Socialist leaders, he became convinced that only the Socialists had a workable program for alleviating the miseries of the laboring classes; so he became a Socialist. The Socialist party in Sweden was intent upon founding a newspaper to express its political beliefs, and Branting was selected to head the enterprise. He established and took over direction of the party's journal *Social Demokraten*.

With nations and with political parties, power is never shared without a struggle. This was true in Sweden where the civil aristocracy and the landed nobility had controlled the government for two hundred years. The editor of *Social Demokraten* was fined for his articles, imprisoned for his editorials, and even threatened with bodily harm. But Branting refused to be silenced. He fought back with all the weapons at his command: an incisive pen, a powerful mind and, of course, his newspaper. And slowly he won converts to his political position. The Socialist party increased in membership and, by 1895, Branting stood on the threshold of a great parliamentary career. Thanks to his wide acquaintance with the rank and file of the Socialist party, whose program appeared to fit the needs of the working class, he won election to the Riksdag and became the first Socialist representative to serve in the Swedish legislature.

In the twenty-nine years of service that lay ahead Branting was a most efficient legislator. Of iron integrity and incorruptible, he led a long and bitter fight to use the power of the state to insure a decent existence for all its citizens. He believed in change resulting from evolution, not revolution. Lucid in argument, logical in thought, and with a viable program at his fingertips, he made the Socialist party a force to be reckoned with.

In 1905, when the union between Norway and Sweden was dissolved and activists in Sweden were shouting for war, Branting, along with Arnoldson, brought to bear his influence as an editor and legislator to stop the talk of war. History credits him with being one of the strong voices in bringing about a peaceful separation of the two nations, enough to warrant a Nobel Prize for Peace.

In all likelihood, though, it was Branting's work with the League of Nations that eventually won him the Prize. Even though Sweden had been neutral during the war that raged between 1914 and 1918, Branting was pro-Ally, largely because he was convinced that the Allies represented civilization and the Germans did not. Even so, as an ardent Socialist he regarded the war as a barbarous block to the growth of international Socialism. In 1916, he was a delegate to the International Socialist Conference at The Hague where a futile attempt was made to bring the fighting to a halt. Finally, when the fighting came to an end, Branting attempted to work out a plan for a democratic peace.

The fact that Branting had been pro-Ally—and the Allies won the war—and that he was an ardent advocate of peace based upon justice, led to his being elected, in 1917, to preside over the preliminary sessions held in preparation for the peace conference of the following year. However, although he early became a convert to the ideas of a League of Nations, he was not to participate in its activities until 1920.

That year, Branting became the first Socialist Prime Minister in the history of Sweden. His Government lasted only from March to October before it was overthrown. But, in 1921, he again formed a Socialist ministry, serving as Prime Minister and as Minister of Foreign Affairs. That same year, he was selected to share the Nobel Prize for Peace with Christian Lange of Norway. Actually, by 1921 Branting had not done much for the cause of peace. It would appear that the Nobel Committee awarded Branting the Prize for work it hoped he would do to bring about world disarmament, a cause in which he *was* vitally interested.

But the hopes of the Committee were not realized, though it was not Branting's fault. In the years between the bestowal of the award and his death in 1925, Branting labored to make the League of Nations an effective organization to keep the peace of the world. He was one of the six vice-presidents of the League of Nations Assembly in 1922; he acted as chairman of the League Disarmament Commission; and he was chairman of the committee that worked out a settlement of the Mosul-Iraq dispute, to name only a few of his activities. But no matter what any one man or many did, it was not enough. Ultimately, mankind will have peace only when it insists upon it.

In January, 1925, Branting became ill and was forced to resign as Prime Minister. A month later, on February 24, he died.

Christian Louis Lange
To Preserve Peace in Time of War

1869–1938

CHRISTIAN LANGE was born on September 17, 1869, at Sta-
vanger, a seaport in southwest Norway. Interested in academic
pursuits, he followed in the footsteps of his grandfather, C.C.A.
Lange, a noted historian and archivist. Endowed with a brilliant
mind, Christian led his class, emerging at graduation with all the
honors. In 1888, he entered the University of Oslo to major in
languages and history.

In 1893 Lange became a teacher, but, much as he enjoyed the
profession, that career ended in 1899, when the Inter-Parliamentary Union met in Oslo and, because of his knowledge of languages

and his ability as an organizer, Lange was appointed secretary of the arrangements committee. He did such a superb job that in 1900 he was offered the position of secretary to the committee newly created by the Storting to award the Peace Prize. For the next years, Lange had an opportunity to become familiar with men who were devoting their lives to peace. He also occupied an important position on the committee appointed to award the Peace Prize, and came to identify completely with the peace movement. Henceforth, as an administrator, writer and lecturer, his efforts focused on the cause of peace.

According to the will drawn up by Alfred Nobel, in addition to a committee which selected the Prize winners, an institute—called the Nobel Institute—was established to help guide the committee in making its selection and to promote all efforts toward peaceful adjustment of disputes among nations. To that end, a library was to be set up, and scholarly and popular educational activities were to be subsidized at home and abroad.

As permanent secretary to a committee whose members changed every few years, much of the work of organizing the Nobel Institute fell upon Lange's shoulders. The most important task performed under his supervision was the research done on the various individuals and organizations nominated for the Prize. The committee members advanced reasons for their choice of candidates, but it was up to the Institute to document the data on nominees.

In the late 1890's, Lange had been active in the movement to effect the political separation of Norway from Sweden. His part in the effort, combined with his work for the Nobel Committee and the Institute, made his name familiar to many of the leading figures in Norwegian politics. In 1907, Lange was appointed one of the delegates to the Second Hague Conference. His uncompromising stand for peace, his forceful arguments delivered in idiomatic French and his engaging personality won the respect and confidence of his colleagues. Two years later that respect and confidence served as the basis for his election to one of the most important positions in the peace movement.

At the Berlin conference of the IPU in 1908, the delegates decided that the work of the IPU Bureau had become too complex for a part-time secretary-general to handle. So in 1909, when Charles Albert Gobat retired, the headquarters of the bureau were transferred from Bern to Brussels and the secretary-general became a full-time, salaried employee. Lange was chosen for the position.

A less capable man than Lange would have found it difficult to follow Gobat. But endowed with a capacity for hard work, Lange directed the fight for peace with consummate skill. He made extended visits to the branches of the IPU; he arranged matters to be taken up by the bureau; he served as a liaison officer between the branches; he edited such bureau publications as the *L'Annuaire de l'Union Inter-parlementaire* and *Documents Inter-parlementaires,* and published numerous articles on the history of the Union.

Even though the Union was temporarily shattered by World War I, the bureau, thanks to Lange, was saved. Taking no chances of having the bureau's records destroyed, Lange moved his headquarters into neutral Norway. From there, he exerted every effort to maintain the lines of communication open between various branches of the union. He kept the organization alive, and even did some preparatory work on projects for a lasting peace once the hostilities came to an end. In 1915, he attended an international pacifist meeting at The Hague and a year later, served as a delegate to the Conference of Neutrals in Stockholm, which sought to bring the war to an end.

There was little money to support the activities of the bureau, or to pay Lange's salary; there wasn't even enough to rent an office. Lange used his living room as an office and supported his family by teaching at the Nobel Institute.

When World War I ended, the exhausted nations turned to the difficult task of establishing an enduring peace. And when the League of Nations came into being, Lange was appointed a delegate to the League Assembly.

For Lange, the major problem facing the League was disarmament; the need, as he put it, to take control of weapons out of the hands of those who would use them to plunge nations into war. War itself, he said, could not be humanized, as the Geneva Convention had tried to do in 1864. It must be suppressed. He contended that nations must disarm or there would always be war.

Some nations did try to disarm; those caught up in a dream of military glory refused. Yet a world at peace appeared possible in the 1920's. In 1921 the IPU, building on the skeleton organization preserved by Lange, once more began its annual conferences with a meeting in Stockholm.

For the secretary-general of the IPU Bureau it was a moment of triumph. Thanks largely to his efforts with the bureau, the union was reborn, and the work of the bureau could go forward.

In December, 1921, Lange received word that the Nobel Committee had selected him to share the Peace Prize with Branting. The receipt of the Prize was merely one of many important episodes in Lange's life. For over a decade he continued as the head of the IPU Bureau; he lectured extensively in the United States and Europe; he wrote and published a number of articles and pamphlets on peace, and he labored indefatigably on the Disarmament Committee of the League of Nations. Finally, in 1933 at the age of sixty-five, he resigned as secretary-general of the bureau.

In 1934, twenty-five years after he resigned as secretary of the Nobel Committee, he was appointed as its member—the only man in the history of the Peace Prize to receive one and to participate in bestowing it upon others.

He died on December 11, 1938, at his home in Oslo.

Fridtjof Nansen
Explorer Turned Humanitarian

1861–1930

FRIDTJOF NANSEN was born at Store-Fröem, on the outskirts of Christiania (now Oslo), on October 10, 1861, into a singularly happy and peaceful home. His father, a clerk for the Norwegian Supreme Court, tended to sternness in supervising his children's activities in school and church, but balanced this by allowing them the widest latitude when it came to roaming through the forests and hills surrounding their home. Fridtjof's mother was almost unique for the times; efficient at taking care of her house and family, she found time to indulge her passion for skiing—considered then a sport for men.

The children were bright and boisterous, and their mother often joined them in their games and adventures. The outdoors called Fridtjof and his brothers. They fished and swam in the nearby river, and roved through the forests, sleeping beneath the trees, getting their food as they needed it; as free as the wild life surrounding them. During the winters, after school, there was ice-skating on the river, fishing through the ice and hunting expeditions on snowshoes.

For a future explorer, it was marvelous training. Fridtjof developed a powerful body capable of withstanding the extreme cold of the North. He learned the art of survival, the unerring sense of direction, the almost intuitive feeling for terrain, which later was to save his life.

When he entered the University of Oslo, in 1880, Fridtjof decided to major in zoology, so that he could do field work, and use his ability to draw. However, for a boy used to the freedom of the woods, the university proved to be boring.

On his way home each day, he frequently crossed the path of a huge, burly man who intrigued him. He learned it was Axel Krifting, a famous Arctic skipper, and that Krifting was on the verge of taking a new sealer, the *Viking*, on her maiden voyage. Nansen introduced himself, impressed Krifting with his earnestness, and joined the crew as student supercargo.

To Nansen the voyage of the *Viking* meant more than just the accumulation of sealskins. The sight of the ice-capped mountains of Greenland aroused in him a desire to do what had never been done: to cross Greenland from coast to coast.

That desire continued to haunt him and, in 1888, he published a plan demonstrating how the feat could be accomplished. He intended to get as close to the eastern shore as possible, abandon the ship, hike across the ice floes and then climb the interior mountains and ski down to the western coast.

Few explorers approved of the plan. The eastern coast was uninhabited. By landing there Nansen would cut himself off from all help; then, he must succeed, or die.

Nansen was daring, but he was no fool. He consulted the old

explorer, Baron Nils Adolph Nordenskjöld, who had conquered the Northeast Passage, but had failed in Greenland. Although Nordenskjöld was skeptical, he gave Nansen some useful advice about equipment. To finance the trip, Nansen turned first to the University of Oslo and then to Parliament, but was refused help. Then a wealthy philanthropist in Copenhagen came to the rescue. His finances assured, Nansen collected a crew of five, packed his equipment and in May, 1888, sailed for Greenland.

At 66° north latitude, Nansen abandoned ship and began the dangerous journey across the ice to shore. He didn't make it. Approximately halfway, the ice broke around him and he and his companions were marooned on a chunk of ice drifting in a southern direction. A prey to wind and current, they drifted three hundred and fifty miles from where they started before their luck changed and the current carried them ashore.

They managed to get back north one hundred and fourteen miles and then turned inland. It was late August—summer was almost over; they had to struggle not only against the elements but against time.

The crossing took thirty-seven days; days of cutting trails up glacier walls, crossing deep crevasses, huddling for warmth in a small tent on days so intensely cold as to freeze a finger or hand if exposed for a moment and cause bitter pain from frostbite. With death as their only alternative, they succeeded and, in September, reached the western coast.

When Nansen and his companions returned to Norway, they received a hero's welcome. They were met at the dock by a committee of the city's leading dignitaries; there were dinners and speeches, and Nansen received several medals. Overnight, he had sprung from obscurity to world fame.

Five years later, in 1893, in a specially designed ship, the *Fram*, Nansen attempted to drift across the North Pole. Within four hundred and fifty miles of his goal, he realized he couldn't succeed. He was too close to give up and decided to make a dash for the Pole with his dogs and sled. Everything went wrong and again he failed. Totally dependent upon his rifle for food, he fought his way south. Winter caught him and he spent the long months of darkness on Frederick Jackson Land. Finally, when spring came, by sheer accident, he met another Arctic expedition and was saved.

Between 1896 and 1917, Nansen devoted most of his time and energy to scientific work. He studied oceanography, published a two-volume account of the Polar expedition (*Furtherest North*) in 1897, participated in the establishment of the International Council for the Exploration of the Sea, and for a time directed the council's central laboratory in Christiania. He also traveled extensively.

In 1905 Nansen took a prominent part in the argument raging over dissolving the union between Norway and Sweden, which Norway overwhelmingly favored. When the separation became a fact and the Norwegian monarchy was established, he was appointed the first ambassador to England.

An internationally known figure, possessing a personality that inspired men's trust and confidence, Nansen was a success as a diplomat. When war broke out in Europe, and Norway found her trade restricted on every side, Nansen was chosen to head a group sent to the United States in search of help. In Washington, he negotiated an agreement whereby America undertook to supply Norway with basic essentials for the remainder of the war.

Norway, like the other Scandinavian countries, maintained a neutral position during World War I. But aware that a future conflagration might engulf them all, the Norwegians wholeheartedly accepted the idea of the League of Nations. In 1920, Nansen was appointed the leader of the Norwegian delegation to the League of Nations.

In Geneva, Nansen immediately assumed a position of leadership. He was appointed by the League as high commissioner and made responsible for the repatriation from Russia of about 500,-000 German and Austro-Hungarian prisoners of war.

Russia, highly suspect because it was Communist, was not a member of the League and consequently did not recognize its existence. But Nansen's reputation was worldwide, and the Russian leaders agreed to negotiate with him. As a result, Nansen reported to the League, in September, 1920, that his task was completed—427,886 prisoners had been repatriated.

This success led Nansen to another important task. In August of 1921, he was asked by the International Red Cross to direct the effort to bring relief to famine-stricken Russia.

Opening an office in Moscow, Nansen plunged into the desperately needed relief work. An appeal for funds from the League was rejected and Nansen was forced into the role of a beggar for his cause. Private organizations extended help. Nansen made personal appeals and managed to raise huge sums of money.

Hundreds of thousands of Russian families were saved from starvation by Nansen's organization. Although he cannot be given complete credit, it was Nansen who directed the relief work, and for his efforts was awarded the Nobel Prize for Peace in 1922.

Prior to his receipt of the Prize Nansen had proposed a far-reaching measure to aid the victims of war. In July, 1922, largely due to Nansen's initiative, an international agreement was reached whereby individuals displaced by the war would be issued a card —later called the "Nansen Passport"—allowing them to move freely across national boundaries when returning to their homes. For a displaced person, the passport was a godsend. Without it, he could easily spend his life being shuttled from one refugee camp to another.

An enthusiastic advocate of arbitration as a means of settling international disputes, Nansen represented Norway on the disarmament committee of the League of Nations in 1927.

In his last years, Norway, in recognition of his many contributions to peace and science, presented him with a country home at Lysaker, just outside of Oslo. There, on May 13, 1930, Fridtjof Nansen died.

The year he died the League of Nations honored Nansen by naming its central refugee service the Nansen International Office for Refugees, which was later a recipient of a Nobel Prize.

Sir Joseph Austen Chamberlain
Easing of International Tensions by Diplomacy

1863–1937

JOSEPH AUSTEN CHAMBERLAIN was born in Birmingham, England, on October 16, 1863. Although his mother died when he was born, Austen's childhood was happy, largely due to the fact that his father, a successful manufacturer and a leader in English politics, spent endless hours with his son, guiding, advising and instructing him, particularly in the world of politics.

Austen attended the best schools: Rugby and then Trinity College, Cambridge, where he took his degree in 1885. Graduation was followed by travel and further study. He toured extensively in France and fell in love with the country. The doors of

Paris society were open to him and Austen met the leaders of the French political world.

Moving on to Berlin, he spent a year listening to lectures at the university and learning to distrust the Germans, whom he found extremely arrogant. When he returned home, thanks to his father's influence and power, he immediately won a seat in the House of Commons, and rose rapidly in the Conservative party, holding several minor posts. Solid rather than brilliant, Chamberlain demonstrated in these positions his capacity for hard work, for painstaking attention to detail and unspectacular, but real political courage. As a result, he continued to advance, becoming, in 1903, Chancellor of the Exchequer.

One of the major tasks of the Chancellor of the Exchequer is the preparation of an annual budget. If the budget fails to win the confidence of the House of Commons, the Government is overthrown and a new one is formed.

Chamberlain prepared two budgets, both of which were well received, but, in 1905, he began to suffer from overwork. Fortunately for him, the Government resigned in December and subsequently was defeated at the polls, though Chamberlain retained his seat in the House of Commons.

In 1906, the Liberals won an overwhelming victory, and as Opposition leader, there was little for Chamberlain to do beyond criticize the Government for what he considered its shortcomings, maneuver to upset the Government and be prepared to take office if he should be successful. He also played a prominent part in inducing Opposition leaders to bring pressure upon the Government to stand by France and Russia in the developing conflict with Germany and Austria.

Then, in the spring of 1915, the long Liberal ascendancy ended. A coalition government was formed and Chamberlain was called in to join it. His fortunes fluctuated, but in 1918 he became a member of Lloyd George's War Cabinet and later that year again became Chancellor of the Exchequer.

In 1921, as leader of the Conservative party, Chamberlain was in a position to be the next Prime Minister when the Conservatives won control of the Government. But he believed that for the present the Lloyd George coalition was essential to England; the rank and file of his party did not. At a conference held in 1922, Chamberlain was voted down. Lacking the confidence of his party, he immediately resigned his leadership.

Passed over in favor of Stanley Baldwin, Chamberlain was out of office during the first Baldwin ministry.

In 1924, he was called in as Secretary of Foreign Affairs. The Labor Prime Minister, James Ramsey MacDonald, who had acted as his own Foreign Secretary, had achieved something of a miracle in winning over the French to the Dawes Plan for clearing the muddle over reparations. The Dawes Plan temporarily financed Germany so she could meet reparation payments. At a meeting of the League of Nations in 1924, MacDonald signed the Geneva Protocol by which the nations involved agreed to accept compulsory jurisdiction of the World Court on questions that seemed to be leading to war. For a moment, these measures met French demands for security and reparations.

However, the MacDonald Government fell and the Geneva Protocol was not ratified by Parliament. Chamberlain opposed it on the grounds that it endangered the freedom of action of the British Commonwealth of Nations. At this juncture, Gustav Stresemann, the German Foreign Minister, came forward with a proposal for a mutual security pact between Germany, France and England. Aristide Briand, the French Foreign Minister, was prepared to negotiate, as was Chamberlain. The result was the seven-nation pact signed at Locarno in 1925.

In barest outline, the pact guaranteed the borders between France and Germany in the region of the Rhine; the nations pledged themselves not to invade each other and to abide by the boundaries established at Versailles; and the German bank of the Rhine was to remain a demilitarized zone. Britain and Italy guaranteed the pledges to the extent of promising aid to the opponent of whoever violated them.

Among the most patient of the Locarno Pact negotiators was Chamberlain. In recognition of his work, the King conferred upon him the Order of the Garter, a distinction only twice before bestowed upon commoners; and in 1925, he was awarded the Nobel Prize for Peace.

After Locarno, Chamberlain's work was done. He remained a Member of Parliament but, with the exception of a few brief months at the Admiralty in 1931, he never again held an administrative post.

Chamberlain died suddenly at his home in London on March 16, 1937.

Charles Gates Dawes
Peace Through Financial Settlement

1865–1951

CHARLES GATES DAWES was born in 1865 into a delightfully quiet world. Marietta, Ohio, established on the spot where the Muskingum joins the Ohio River, was in all essentials a small New England town. The early settlers in the region laid out the village, built their homes and their churches, and established grammar schools, high schools and a college.

Charles was graduated from Marietta College, fourth in his class. He then entered Cincinnati Law School, where he compiled a fine record. When he had acquired his law degree, he went west to Lincoln, Nebraska, to practice.

In 1887 Lincoln was a boom town. Seemingly it was an ideal place to begin a law career, but there was one drawback: keen competition. During his early months in Lincoln, Dawes had to struggle just to survive. Gradually, however, he became more and more successful. Meanwhile, William Jennings Bryan, later to be three-time candidate for the Presidency, had become a close personal friend, as had Lieutenant John J. Pershing, who was to lead the United States forces in Europe in World War I. A shrewd businessman, Dawes made investments for his friends and profited himself, financially and in terms of business experience.

By 1893 Dawes was well on his way to modest wealth. Then disaster struck and the country was plunged into depression. Lincoln became, economically, a ghost town, and within two years Dawes owed over $200,000.

Borrowing from friends and using what remained of his savings, Dawes invested in several Chicago companies and in 1895, he moved there. His investments were profitable and he was soon able to pay his debts in full.

A friendly man with good connections, and a noted lawyer, Dawes rapidly became one of the outstanding bankers of his day. In 1902 he noted in his diary, "I am now worth . . . something over $400,000, above all my liabilities." For a man who had owed over $200,000, he was doing well.

Although a banker, Dawes' interests ranged beyond just making money. In the panic of 1907, when the specter of want hovered over the city, he was instrumental in having fed between 30,000 and 40,000 people during the winter. His charities were legion in an era when there was no government help. But, according to Dawes, he had no charities, he just helped a few people.

With the beginning of the war in Europe in 1914, Dawes' life changed, as did the lives of most Americans. In May, 1917, the fifty-one year old Dawes left his business to enter the Army. He was much too old, but his powerful friend, Commander of the American Expeditionary Forces, John J. Pershing, managed to commission him a major.

But he was not to see action. Pershing appointed him head of the General Purchasing Board of the United States Army in Europe. It was an important position—he had to coordinate with the French and English the flow of provisions to the front and make sure the fighting men had all the supplies they needed. Dawes was extremely successful and emerged from the war a general.

By 1920 Dawes was a national figure. After the election of 1920, Warren Harding offered to appoint him Secretary of the Treasury, but Dawes refused. He did accept a newly created position, Director of the Budget, with the understanding he would only stay long enough to organize the office. In 1922, convinced that the Budget Bureau was functioning smoothly, he retired to private life—temporarily.

Dawes' sense of responsibility once more lured him from the world of business. In 1923, he accepted a job as head of a committee to stabilize the European economy.

When Germany collapsed in 1918, the victorious Allies imposed upon her the obligation of paying for the entire war. France and England were dependent upon German payments to repay war loans from the United States and to rebuild their own economies. They found themselves in an extremely tight position financially since Germany could not pay. Then the German economy collapsed completely and Europe was thrown into chaos. Dawes and his committee were to rectify the situation, if possible.

It was an infinitely complex task. The committee had to decide how much Germany could afford to pay and these payments had to be balanced against French and English demands. The German economy had to be bolstered by loans from the United States.

Partially due to his capacity for hard work and mastery of detail, and his willingness to compromise and accept suggestions, Dawes succeeded. By April, 1924, a plan was worked out and agreed upon by Germany and the other nations. The economy of Europe was stabilized upon a much firmer foundation.

Returning to the United States with the title of "The Savior of Europe," Dawes was plunged into politics. In 1924 he was elected Vice-President of the United States.

In 1925, for the great service he had rendered Europe and the world, Dawes was named co-winner of the Nobel Prize for Peace with Austen Chamberlain. It is indicative of the man that there is no mention in his diary of the award and that he turned over the Prize money to the Walter Hines Page School of International Relations.

At the conclusion of his four years in the Vice-Presidency, Dawes was asked by President Herbert Hoover to serve as American ambassador to England. He was well-known to many of England's leading statesmen and the United States was trying to arrive at an understanding with England over armaments. As in his other roles, Dawes was successful. In 1930 the Senate ratified an armaments treaty between the two countries.

Dawes spent four months as president of the Reconstruction Finance Corporation and then he retired.

His last years were extremely happy. He enjoyed good health and had a multitude of business interests and a well-stocked library. It was in his library, the evening of April 23, 1951, that he greeted his wife with a smile and then, leaning back in his chair, closed his eyes and died.

Aristide Briand
France and Locarno

1862–1932

ARISTIDE BRIAND was born on March 28, 1862, in Nantes, a town in the district of the Loire. His father owned a small inn patronized by petty tradesmen, farmers from the surrounding region and itinerants: musicians, artists and workers drifting from town to town.

Gifted at caricature, young Aristide delighted his father's guests by doing their portraits in charcoal and, if that palled, by exhibiting his genius for mimicry. His voice charged with emotion, he would convulse the guests with laughter as he addressed an imaginary judge and jury on behalf of an imaginary defendant. It was all great fun, but unconsciously he was developing the talents that would one day make him "the greatest master of debate in the world."

Blessed with a marvelous speaking voice, he decided to become a lawyer and succeeded because the qualifications weren't very rigorous. He wasn't the most diligent of students; he lived, in fact, a Bohemian life, drinking, talking, and playing cards. He also became a Socialist and contributed articles on Socialism to radical newspapers.

At the age of twenty he founded a newspaper, *La Democratie de l 'Ouest,* and although it failed, the venture whetted a taste for journalism that never left him. For many years, even after he had become involved in politics, he continued to maintain a connection with the publishing world.

Returning to law practice, he opened an office in St. Nazaire and waited for clients. Few came, so he used his leisure to study social problems and engage in work for the Socialist party. Eventually, party work absorbed his full attention and he gave up the practice of law entirely.

Briand began as a protagonist of extremism. An advocate of the general strike, collectivism and direct action, he soon mustered a considerable following within the party. His talents as a propagandist were recognized, and he was made secretary-general.

In 1902 Briand was elected to the Chamber of Deputies. In the Chamber he established a reputation as a master of debate and an orator without peer. He was also an able politician who understood the value of compromise and the necessity of standing firm when vital issues were involved. It was no surprise when Briand was called upon in July, 1909, to form his own Cabinet.

When he became Prime Minister, Briand announced he would adopt a policy of national understanding and tranquillity. The policy, however, was in force less than a year. In his youth Briand had preached that the general strike was a weapon labor could use to force the Government to acceed to its demands. Now in 1910 labor called a general railroad strike and threatened France with paralysis.

Briand's answer to the challenge was ruthless and uncompromising. Proclaiming the strike a revolutionary plot to overthrow the state, he issued a mobilization order placing the strikers under the jurisdiction of the Army. Members of the strike committee were arrested; the rank and file of workers—if they refused to obey orders—were fired. Briand broke the strike.

One result of his action was a terrific storm in the Chamber of Deputies. Assailed by the left as a traitor and renegade, he replied that the Government had to break the strike because the railroads were indispensable to national defense and to national existence. But his majority in the Chamber withered away and he resigned as Premier.

In 1921, at a most inauspicious moment, Briand was again called upon to form his own ministry. Two major problems, German reparations and defense, were agitating the Chamber of Deputies, and if the Prime Minister failed to solve them, he was sure to fall. Taking charge of foreign affairs, Briand first applied himself to the question of reparations. France had suffered terribly in the war and no man could survive in French politics unless he were committed to a policy that Germany must pay. But how much? In 1921 the Reparations Committee had pegged the figure at thirty-three billion dollars, a fantastic amount in terms of the German economy.

Through the spring and summer of 1921, since it was obvious that Germany could *not* pay, Briand recognized that it would be necessary to grant her a limited moratorium. But the Chamber, intent upon a "pay now" policy, would be certain to view the moratorium in a most unfavorable light.

Early in 1922 Briand found his position completely untenable. After a meeting with Britain's Lloyd George to discuss the reparations problem and to attempt to negotiate a treaty whereby England would guarantee France's borders, Briand returned to Paris to find himself being bitterly criticized because he had played golf with Lloyd George! Disgusted, Briand resigned from the ministry.

In 1925, Briand accepted the portfolio of Foreign Affairs and began the series of negotiations that led to the Locarno agreements. An immediate result of Locarno was the easing of tensions on France's eastern frontier. Having achieved in 1925 what he had failed to achieve in 1922—the British guarantee of French security —Briand gained an enormous reputation in French politics as an able negotiator. The treaties, apparently assuring the peace of Europe into the distant future, were hailed as diplomatic triumphs by the leaders of other nations and, in 1926, for his leading role in the negotiations, Briand shared the Nobel Prize for Peace with Gustav Stresemann of Germany.

For a few months Briand was again Prime Minister and then Minister of Foreign Affairs, a position he held through the rise and fall of various governments (including another one of his own) for the next five years. During that time, he engaged in a series of negotiations that continued to bring him to the attention of the world.

Following World War I, many leading Americans became convinced that war between nations should be outlawed. Briand was contacted, and on April 6, 1927, the tenth anniversary of American entry into World War I, he delivered an address to the American people in which he asserted that "France would be ready publicly to subscribe, with the United States, to any mutual engagement tending, as between those two countries, to 'outlaw war.' "

Under the existing political conditions in the United States, a bilateral pact was impossible, so Frank Kellogg, the United States Secretary of State, countered with the suggestion that the pact be multilateral. This was acceptable to Briand, and on August 17, 1928, fifteen nations met in Paris to affix their signatures to what came to be called the Paris Peace Pact, or, the Kellogg-Briand Pact. The fifteen nations—later to be joined by most of the nations of the world—agreed on a policy among themselves to resolve all their difficulties by pacific means.

The years of unrelenting political activity and responsibility had aged Briand beyond his years. Tired and overworked, the man who had been Prime Minister of France eleven times died in Paris on March 7, 1932.

Gustave Stresemann
Germany and Locarno

1878–1929

GUSTAVE STRESEMANN, the future Chancellor of the Weimar Republic, was born in the ancient Prussian capital of Berlin on May 10, 1878. His father was what we would call today a middleman; that is, he accepted consignments of beer from the brewers, bottled and distributed it. The business was profitable, and young Stresemann grew up in a comfortable household.

At the gymnasium Stresemann was one of the top students in his class, and he easily won admission to the University of Berlin in 1897.

His career at the university was typical of the intellectually oriented German student of that period. He involved himself in campus politics and was elected speaker of a student association. He fought for the principle that no student should be excluded from the university because of race, and he won. More important, in terms of his personal career, he was such a diligent student that, in his early twenties, he was awarded a Ph.D.

Stresemann found a position almost immediately as an assistant in the management of the Association of German Chocolate Manufacturers, where he quickly demonstrated his ability as a brilliant organizer.

Stresemann's interest in politics came as a direct result of his work with the association. He often had reason to fight its battles in the lower chamber of the Saxon parliament, and developed a taste for politics which led to his election to the Reichstag in 1907.

Because of a bad heart, Stresemann was not called for military service in World War I. However, he spent the war years bending every effort to further the ends of the armed services and became thoroughly identified with the military aims of Germany.

As a result of the shattering political upheavals that followed the armistice in November, 1918, Stresemann's party, the National Liberal party, collapsed. Unable to win admission to the party of his choice because of his war record, Stresemann turned to the great industrialists and put together the German People's party.

Backed by the industrialists and guided by Stresemann, the People's party became the arbiter of German politics in the postwar years. However, the business interests in Germany didn't involve themselves in the affairs of the party out of pure altruism. Certain demands had to be met. Foreign loans were needed, and to get loans, business leaders abroad had to be confident that Germany was again peaceful. Thus Stresemann was forced by circumstances into what came to be known as a policy of "fulfillment."

The Versailles Treaty had compelled Germany to promise she would meet the reparations demands imposed upon her. The peace treaty was thought grossly unfair by the German people and their leaders. But Germany was in an extremely delicate position.

Her borders were undefended, the political situation was unstable and business needed foreign help. Stresemann, and other leaders, realized that something would have to be done to meet the demands of the Allies. Thus Stresemann espoused a policy of conditional fulfillment; that is, Germany would fulfill some demands and insist on certain compensations. But at the London Conference in 1921, Germany was hit with a bill for about thirty-three billion dollars. With her chaotic economic condition Germany defaulted on her payments, and France decided to use force. In 1923, France and Belgium invaded the Ruhr.

There was little Germany could do, except adopt a policy of passive resistance. Within a few months it became obvious that the economy could not stand the strain of passive resistance or of being deprived of the materials produced in the Ruhr. The value of the mark fell incredibly low and eventually it took billions of marks to equal one dollar. Then came Stresemann's moment. He was called upon to form a Cabinet.

It was a bad time to be made Chancellor. Currency was worthless and the French refused to evacuate the Ruhr until passive resistance came to an end. Stresemann himself was suspect by parties on both the left and the right because he came to power pledged to a policy of conditional fulfillment and because his was the party of big business.

His Chancellorship lasted three months, but it was a turning point in the fortunes of the Weimar Republic. Moving swiftly, he abandoned the passive resistance movement in the Ruhr and, by mortgaging Germany's entire resources, acted to stabilize the currency, a major step in encouraging American aid.

Upon the fall of his government in November, 1923, Stresemann accepted the portfolio of Foreign Minister in the new Cabinet of Wilhelm Marx and set about developing peaceful relations with Germany's neighbors. He was perfectly aware that as long as France feared a future attack from Germany and as long as Germany was threatened by a repetition of the Ruhr invasion, there was no possibility of the pacification of Europe; a necessary first step was settling the reparations problem.

In 1924 Stresemann, as a member of the German delegation to London to resolve the reparations issue, quickly established himself as one of the dominant personalities at the conference. The negotiations, by and large, resulted in a victory for Germany with the initiation of the Dawes Plan. Stresemann was then free to deal with the equally large problem of working out some kind of a mutual security pact with France. In early 1925, he sent a formal note to Paris, suggesting a mutual guarantee by England, France and Germany of the postwar Franco-German frontier against aggression on either side.

The note was barely acknowledged by either France or England. Then Briand came to power as French Foreign Minister. He, too, was concerned about the unending animosity between Germany and France and hence receptive to Stresemann's idea. Chamberlain was won over, with the result that the foreign ministers of Germany, France and England met at Locarno, Switzerland, and drew up the terms of the mutual security pact.

By the Locarno Pact, Germany, France and Belgium pledged themselves not to change their existing frontiers by a resort to arms. The treaties were to go into effect upon Germany's admission to the League of Nations. Thus, with the backing of the other treaty nations, Stresemann led a large German delegation to Geneva in 1926 to take part in the impressive ceremonies that once more saw Germany as an equal among the nations of Europe.

By 1926 Stresemann was being hailed as Europe's leading politician, and when he was awarded the Nobel Prize for Peace, there were few who questioned either Stresemann's merits or the giving of the award.

The Locarno Pact and the Prize were the twin capstones of his career. His health had been broken by overwork in the crucial years between 1923 and 1926, but he labored on as Foreign Secretary. On October 3, 1929, he suffered an apoplectic stroke and died.

Ferdinand Buisson
World's Most Persistent Pacifist

1841–1932

FERDINAND BUISSON, the oldest man to ever win a Nobel Prize for Peace, was born on December 20, 1841, in Paris. Little is known of his early years, except that he attended the University of Paris.

Buisson hoped to be a teacher, but he would not take the required oath of loyalty to the Emperor, Napoleon III, who was little better than a dictator. He moved to Switzerland where, between 1866 and 1870, he was a professor at the academy at Neuchâtel.

Buisson was an early advocate of peace. In 1867 he had joined with Frédéric Passy, Giuseppe Garibaldi and others in the creation of the famous peace organization, the *Ligue Internationale de la Paix et de la Liberté*. But it was not really until the 1890's that he again became active in the peace movement. Of immediate interest to him was the French defeat in the Franco-Prussian War with the resultant overthrow of Napoleon III and the establishment of the Third Republic.

When Buisson returned to France in 1870, he met Jules Simon, the newly appointed Minister of Public Instruction. Impressed by Buisson's intelligence, energy, and dedication to education, Simon named him Inspector of Primary Education in Paris. But Buisson's convictions that education in France must be removed from the control of the Catholic Church were not acceptable to the National Assembly, and his appointment was not confirmed. Fortunately, the conservative reaction that had followed the fall of Napoleon abated toward the end of the decade, and, in 1878, Buisson was named inspector general of all the elementary schools in France. The following year he moved up to Director of Elementary Education in the Ministry of Public Instruction.

In 1896 Buisson resigned his government post to become professor of the science of education at the Sorbonne. In the next several years he taught, published a number of books and articles, and became indirectly involved in the Dreyfus Affair, a major political event in French history.

The case began in 1894 when Captain Alfred Dreyfus, accused of giving military secrets to the Germans, was arrested and charged with treason. Tried by secret court-martial, he was condemned and sent to Devil's Island. To put it bluntly, he was framed. The press had suspected a traitor on the General Staff and the Army needed a scapegoat. Dreyfus, a Jew, intensely hated by most of his conservative colleagues who were Catholic, royalist and anti-Semitic, was an obvious choice. Even when new evidence, which tended to prove Dreyfus' innocence, was presented to the Army, nothing was done. Then in 1898 Émile Zola, the famous novelist, published an open letter, *J'Accuse*, which caused a sensation and reopened the case. Eventually, Dreyfus was found to be innocent. The government released him, gave him a medal and promoted him to major.

The same year Zola published his famous letter, Buisson, convinced that Dreyfus was innocent, joined with a few men in founding the League of the Rights of Man which subsequently became an important force in securing justice for other innocent men in France. As much to the point, his political sensibilities aroused, Buisson gave up his secure position at the Sorbonne to run for the Chamber of Deputies in 1902. He won and so began a political career that extended, with some interruptions, until 1924.

Actually, Buisson did not have a great parliamentary career. Very little was heard about him until 1923, when France invaded the Ruhr. He was then eighty-two years old.

But, as on earlier occasions, his conscience would not let him stand by and do nothing about the hatred being generated by conflict in the Ruhr. He bitterly attacked French policy in an effort to bring about a rapprochement with Germany. He invited German pacifists to Paris and he went to Germany to speak in Mainz and Berlin. Everywhere the burden of his message was the same: there must be a reconciliation between France and Germany, as the peace of Europe, indeed, the peace of the world, depended upon it. As he expressed it:

There is something which is above France, above Germany, above all nations: that is humanity. But above humanity is that justice which finds its most perfect manifestation in human fraternity.

Buisson's was a magnificent effort for peace on the part of a man past his eightieth year and, in 1927, the Nobel Committee awarded him the Prize. On February 15, 1932, he died in Paris.

Ludwig Quidde
Exiled Antimilitarist

1858–1941

LUDWIG QUIDDE, who shared the Prize with Ferdinand Buisson of France in 1927, was born into a wealthy merchant family in Bremen, Germany, on March 23, 1858. His keen mind flourished in school; he was graduated with honors and gained admittance to the University of Strassburg.

For no clear reason, Quidde did not take a university degree. Interested in history, after study at Strassburg and the University of Göttingen, he became the editor of *Deutsche Reichstagsakten*, founded and edited another journal, *Zeitschrift für Geschichtewissenschaft* and served as secretary of the Prussian Historical Institute in Rome from 1890 to 1892. He might have made a name in the academic world had he not become involved in the cause of peace.

In 1891, when Bertha von Suttner founded the German Peace Society, Quidde became a convert. In 1894 he himself founded a peace group in Munich, over which he presided until 1918 and, convinced that peace must have an advocate in German politics, he became in time a member of the National Assembly.

However, his most striking efforts to further the cause of peace in this period were a violent attack upon the military, published anonymously in 1893, and a pamphlet, only some twenty pages in length, written and published under his own name in 1894. Entitled *Caligula: A Study in Roman Caesarean Madness*, the pamphlet, while pretending to be a serious historical study (and it was quite accurate historically), was a thinly veiled satire on the posturings and pretensions of Kaiser Wilhelm II. The pamphlet caused a storm of controversy. Some were delighted by Quidde's boldness in publishing the attack; others thought him a traitor and Quidde was put in jail. When brought to trial, he was acquitted of libel and the case was dropped.

By the turn of the century, Quidde had become famous in the international peace movement. A member of the directing commission of the Bureau International de la Paix, in 1905, at the World Peace Congress held in Lucerne, Switzerland, he joined with Frédéric Passy in an attempt to bring about Franco-German conciliation. Unsuccessful, two years later he tried again, and again failed. The two nations wanted peace with honor, and their notions of honor failed to correspond. Elected to the Bavarian Landtag (second chamber) in 1907, he became a member of the Inter-Parliamentary Union a year later, participating thereafter in a number of Inter-Parliamentary conferences.

An attempt on Quidde's part in 1913 to bring an end to the armaments race, in which all the major powers of Europe were involved, was already too late. War came in the late summer of 1914. Forced, because of his pacifism, to live in Switzerland during World War I, Quidde maintained an extensive correspondence with pacifists in both the neutral and belligerent nations, and in 1915, he was the German delegate to a meeting at The Hague to end the war.

Finally in 1918, Quidde was able to return to Germany. And he was free to return to politics. In 1919 he was elected Deputy in the German National Assembly. Although he believed that Germany must assume a large share of responsibility for the war, he was against the Versailles Treaty because it fixed the guilt solely upon Germany. But Quidde *was* convinced that the future peace of the world rested with the League of Nations and that Germany must join and use her strength to promote international peace.

A peaceful Germany, honestly attempting to live up to her treaty obligations, would have to avoid any attempt to rearm. In the years immediately after the war, however, secret groups were trained, an air force was built and Germany's treaty obligations were violated on every side.

Through his connections with peace workers in Germany, Quidde was aware of the development of these secret organizations and he published a series of newspaper articles exposing them and their ties to the Government. As a result of the articles Quidde was arrested and accused of "collaborating with the enemy." It was not an easy charge to prove, and the Government failed. The fact that such a charge could be brought against Quidde in itself indicated the atmosphere in which German pacifists had to work.

In 1927, for his long and arduous service in the cause of peace, Ludwig Quidde was awarded the Nobel Prize. Most Germans greeted the award with derisive jeers.

In 1933 Adolph Hitler became Chancellor, and in Hitler's Germany there was no place for men who won Nobel Prizes for Peace. Quidde was forced into exile again and died on March 4th, 1941, in Geneva, Switzerland.

Frank B. Kellogg
Treaty to Outlaw War

1856–1937

In October, 1865, a nine-year-old boy joined his younger brother and sister in the family wagon and watched as his father shook the reins loose about the horses' necks. Like many thousands of others, the Kelloggs were heading west. Ending their journey in Minnesota, they settled first on a small farm near Viola, and then on a larger one near the town of Elgin.

As the Kelloggs had discovered back in New York State—where Frank was born in Potsdam on December 22, 1856—farm life was hard, and it continued to be hard even on the rich farm lands of Minnesota, particularly since Asa Kellogg was ill part of the time. Frank enjoyed few of the amenities of life. However, he was taught at home by his mother and did manage to attend school for a few months, which was the only formal schooling he ever had. Even so, it was enough to whet his determination to become a lawyer.

The question was how. Fortunately, his younger brother was content to stay on the farm, and his father's health improved, with the result that when Frank was nineteen he was free to enter a law office in Rochester, Minnesota. He received no salary, but he had the run of the office, the use of the law books and the encouragement and advice of his mentor. Despite the difficulties of mere survival, plus those of adequate preparation, he passed his bar examinations in 1877.

Comparatively speaking, Frank Kellogg rose rapidly in his profession. In 1878 he was elected city attorney of Rochester; and in 1881 he was elected county attorney, a much more responsible position. However, the turning point in his career came when the town of Elgin retained him as counsel in a case involving the Winona-St. Peter Railroad.

It was a big case in those days for a young man only some seven years a lawyer. Kellogg studied the facts meticulously and, in spite of the railroad's expert legal advice, he won the case. For Frank Kellogg, this victory produced two important results: It increased his reputation enormously and it brought him a partnership in a St. Paul law firm.

Having succeeded in the state court, Kellogg was ready to move toward the wider horizons of corporate law. Paradoxically, since his reputation was at least partially established by a legal victory over a railroad, he became an attorney for some of the more important ones around St. Paul. He also acted as counsel for such great corporations as the United States Steel Company and the Minnesota Iron Company.

In 1900 he was approached by the editor and manager of the *St. Paul Pioneer Press* and asked to act as counsel in a suit to be brought against the General Paper Company for violating the Sherman Anti-Trust Act of 1890. Again, he was successful. The verdict received nation-wide publicity and brought Kellogg to the attention of President Theodore Roosevelt, who recruited him to act against giant corporations attempting to create nation-wide monopolies.

On the national level, Kellogg's outstanding accomplishment was in the suit brought against the Standard Oil Company—a corporation thought to be so huge that even the Federal Government would be unsuccessful in any attempt to control its activities. But in 1911, the Supreme Court upheld decisions made in the lower courts; the corporation was declared a monopoly and ordered dissolved.

In 1916, Kellogg accepted the nomination of the Republican party for a senate seat and carried the state by a large majority. His years in the Senate were uneventful. From 1916 to 1918 the war commanded his attention, and after the war he was engrossed with the peace settlement.

The war and its aftermath had one unfortunate consequence for Kellogg. He failed to campaign as energetically as he had in 1916, and was defeated for reelection in 1922.

Kellogg prepared to resume his law practice, but President Warren G. Harding intervened. The President selected him to attend the Fifth Pan-American Conference in Santiago, Chile. Shortly thereafter, he was offered the post of ambassador to England, which he reluctantly accepted.

The year in London, as Ambassador to the Court of St. James's, was an exciting one. The Kelloggs made numerous friends, and Kellogg was able to render meritorious service to his country on several occasions.

Shortly after President Calvin Coolidge's election in 1924, Ambassador Kellogg received a cable from the State Department. The retiring Secretary of State had suggested to the President that Kellogg be nominated to succeed him.

Frank Kellogg's four years as Secretary of State can be succinctly summed up as a search for peace. Although the United States did not join the League of Nations in the 1920's, it joined in every major effort to limit the amount of armaments each nation could possess. And in 1928 it joined with France in trying to promote peace for all time through the Kellogg-Briand Pact.

On August 27, 1928, representatives of Britain, her Dominions, Germany, Poland, Czechoslovakia, Japan and Belgium joined with France and the United States in signing the pact. The signatories, it was stated, "solemnly declare . . . that they condemn recourse to war as an instrument of national policy in their relations with one another." Simultaneously with the signing of the treaty, other nations were invited to join. Response was quick. Within ten days, twenty-five states signified their interest. Eventually, a hundred and three nations signed the pact.

This was the culmination of Frank Kellogg's career, the incident of which he was most proud. Resigning as Secretary of State in 1929, he was invited to become a judge in the World Court, a position of great dignity and honor. While acting as a judge he received notice that he had been awarded the Nobel Prize for 1929. The award affected him deeply. "It is the highest honor any man could receive," he said. He accepted the Prize in Norway. Although in his seventies, he had no thought of retiring; he carried on his work in the Permanent Court of International Justice until ill health forced him to resign in 1935. He died at his home in St. Paul in 1937.

Nathan Söderblom
Peace Through Christianity

1866–1931

NATHAN SÖDERBLOM was born on January 15, 1866, into a home ardently devoted to Christian principles. A Lutheran minister, Nathan's father modeled his life after Christ and required that his family follow his example. All that Christ had asked for was food and clothing, so there was little beyond that and a few pieces of furniture in the Söderblom home. However, there was love and a tradition that emphasized the training of the mind.

Beginning in the provincial town of Hudiksvall and progressing through a series of other schools in small towns, Nathan's education reached out to broad horizons when he entered the

University of Upsala in 1883. This was the period in Sweden when the university was aflame with new ideas, old values were being challenged on every side and ancient beliefs regarded with deep suspicion.

This welling up of intellectual excitement at the university made a deep impression on the young provincial. He developed a deep and abiding interest in the great German reformer, Martin Luther. A gifted linguist, he acquired knowledge of the languages of the Middle East which, in turn, led to formal studies in the religions of that area. In attempting to trace the relationships existent between religions, he became an expert in the field of comparative religion. But, while his religious views were modified by his studies, his faith never changed and remained a fundamental part of his life.

When, in 1886, he was graduated with honors in classical and oriental languages, Söderblom immediately began to study for the Doctor of Divinity degree. First, however, he took a degree in theology—in 1892—and the following year was ordained in the Lutheran Church. That year he also published a book entitled *The Religion of Luther*, began an intensive study of the Iranian language and started work on his dissertation for a Ph.D. But, at the same time, he had to find a way to support himself. In 1894, he accepted a position as chaplain to the Swedish legation in Paris, which also included the care of the Swedish congregation in the city.

One of his more fruitful contacts in Paris was with Alfred Nobel. The millionaire had little use for organized religion himself, but he recognized Söderblom's sincerity, admired his learning, and responded generously when Söderblom asked for funds to help support the church in Paris. In a sense Söderblom repaid his generosity; he officiated at Nobel's elaborate funeral on December 29, 1896.

In 1901, thirty-five-year-old Söderblom, with a doctorate from the University of Paris, returned to the University of Upsala as a professor of theology. A gifted teacher, Söderblom brought about a revival of interest in religion among the students and faculty. His warm, vibrant personality drew students into his classes, his mastery of subject matter impressed them; his eloquence and conviction were persuasive. Moreover, though a convinced Christian himself, he was not dogmatic. Based on his own research into the religions of the past, he was prepared to believe there was some measure of truth in most. He generated enthusiasm, and other faculty members, awakened to new challenges and opportunities, rallied to make the Department of Theology one of the best on campus. In spite of his busy life, Söderblom found time to write. *The Religion of Revelation* was published in 1903, and two years later, *The Religions of the World.* In 1910 he published *The Religious Problem in Catholicism and Protestantism,* and in 1914, *Origin of the Belief in God.* During this time he also published nearly a hundred articles. His reputation as a scholar grew perhaps even more rapidly than his fame as a teacher and minister.

Late in 1913, when the Archbishop of Upsala died, leaving vacant the leading church position in Sweden, the King decided to name Söderblom as his successor. Technically, even if he was the only Archbishop in Sweden, Söderblom was just first among equals; each bishop in the Swedish church was to a degree ecclesiastically independent. But Söderblom came to occupy a position of great authority and prestige. He made the church an integral part of Swedish life, as well as a symbol of truth and justice. More than that, both inside and outside of Sweden he became known as a champion of church unity and of world peace.

In 1914, long before he became head of the Swedish church, Söderblom was one of the founders of a General World Union of Churches for International Understanding. Unfortunately, World War I interrupted and then ended the work of the union, despite the efforts of Söderblom and other Scandinavian clerics to keep it alive.

In 1917, along with other clergymen from neutral countries, the Archbishop attempted to arrange a general conference of churches, again designed to promote world brotherhood. However, as in 1914, the bitter passions aroused by the war were such that the authorities refused to grant the necessary passports.

A small meeting, composed largely of Scandinavian churches, met at Upsala in September, 1917. As host and guiding spirit of the proceedings, Söderblom was to some degree responsible for the issuance of a manifesto. In it the disturbing discrepancy between a world at war and the teachings of Christ was clearly delineated, and the manifesto urged the church, in the broadest nondenominational sense, to take a more active role in reducing that discrepancy and hopefully one day eliminating it.

Söderblom was a pacifist, and he was fully convinced that organized religion could and should play a vital role in preventing the outbreak of future conflict. In 1920 he was able to convoke a meeting in Geneva which laid the foundation for an ecumenical gathering to be held in Stockholm in 1925.

This meeting, called the Universal Christian Conference on Life and Work, was the culmination of Söderblom's career in international peace and Christian cooperation. More than six hundred delegates from thirty-seven countries attended, and only the Roman Catholic Church was not represented among the major Christian communities. The conference accomplished a great deal, especially in paving the way for future internationally minded ecumenical gatherings. This was the result of Söderblom's diligent planning and organizational work in advance of the conference, and his constant encouragement during the meetings. Subsequent gatherings, built upon the solid foundation laid by this conference, resulted in the formation of the World Council of Churches.

The greatest event of Söderblom's last years was winning the Nobel Prize for Peace in 1930—a well-deserved award. He had spent a large portion of his life promoting universal peace through Christian unity, based upon the concept of the brotherhood of man. That the churches, particularly after 1925, engaged themselves in the attempt to bring wars to an end was due in large measure to his activities.

Enjoying good health most of his life, Söderblom developed heart trouble in 1926, and after carrying on his exacting duties for a few years, he died on July 12, 1931.

Jane Addams
Humanitarian and Pacifist

1860–1935

In the shadow of great Norwegian pines in a little cemetery just outside of Cedarville, Illinois, there lies a simple grave. Carved into the headstone are the words: Jane Addams of Hull House and the Women's International League for Peace and Freedom.

The words, in their unadorned simplicity, conceal the greatness of the name and the fame attached to it. Yet, the stone bears a fitting epitaph. Jane Addams, Hull House and Peace and Freedom are so inextricably entwined that to speak of one is to mean all three.

Born in 1860 into the large family of John Addams, she was surrounded from birth by culture, honor and integrity. Her father was a wealthy miller, a state senator and a friend of Abraham Lincoln. He was an individual endowed with wide learning, deep convictions, tolerance and understanding.

Jane Addams was a shy, withdrawn child. Born with a curved spine and prone to abscesses, until her mid-twenties she knew almost constant pain and was forced to walk with her head slightly tilted forward and to one side. For a sensitive child, this resulted in a feeling of inferiority, of being "different."

Her ill health and the example of her father served to interest her in books at an early age. Knowing that her father rose punctually at 3 A.M. and read until dawn, she decided to do the same, involving herself in a course of reading which included history, literature, novels and plays.

It was no surprise that she did well in school. When she was graduated from Rockford College in the spring of 1881, she was class president and valedictorian. But then what? She could not contemplate marriage since it was physically impossible for her to have children; she had no particular interest in becoming a foreign missionary, as some educated women did.

Etching the future in even darker shadows was the loss of her greatest source of strength and security. Her mother had died when she was a baby and, just before her twenty-first birthday, her father died of a burst appendix. To stay in Cedarville, in the house where her father had lived, was impossible. In the fall of 1881 she enrolled in the Women's Medical College in Philadelphia.

For a few months she did very well and then her health broke completely and she was an invalid for almost two years. In 1883, her doctor prescribed a trip to Europe, and Jane Addams began a lengthy tour of the Continent. This was the usual cultural tour of a well-educated, well-to-do young lady of the period: visits to cathedrals, art museums and historic sites.

It was while on a second trip to Europe some years later that Miss Addams was to settle on her life's work. A few years before, a group of Oxford students had established Toynbee Hall in the Whitechapel district of London. The students believed that social evils could only be eradicated by direct action and by personal involvement. They lived among the poor, met them on a person-to-person basis, came to understand their problems and attempted to create a bridge of hope between the two extremes of society.

Jane Addams studied Toynbee Hall, where she found what she was looking for—a practical way to be of service. She returned to the United States determined to found her own settlement house, and discovered the ideal location in the slums of Chicago.

Hull House, originally built in 1856 as a private residence, is a beautifully proportioned, two-story brick structure. When Jane Addams rented the upper floor in 1889, the lower floor was half-saloon and half-storage room and office of a furniture factory. At the time of her death in 1935, the settlement had spread to include an entire block, a striking example of what can be done when vision and hard work are blended with driving determination.

And Jane Addams worked hard, often beyond the limits of her strength. Her own resources were limited to some three thousand dollars a year, and she was constantly involved in a struggle for economic survival. Taking advantage of every opportunity, she spoke to groups explaining what she was attempting to do, and gradually donations began to come in. At all hours of the night and day, she was out on errands of mercy, sometimes helping to deliver a child, sometimes sitting with the dying. She organized classes where the poor could study everything from art to cooking. Although she was surrounded by men and women no less dedicated than herself, she was always the focal point, and hers the responsibility.

In the first year of its existence, fifty thousand people came to Hull House for help, and during its second year, over one hundred thousand. The House became for many an oasis of hope in a dreary, monotonous life. Here the newly arrived immigrant could learn English, his wife how to shop and his daughter how to make her own dresses. Here the destitute could find someone who cared. It is no wonder that many considered Jane Addams a saint.

She was certainly always a fighter for just causes. At Hull House's first Christmas party, she found little girls rejecting candy because they worked fourteen hours a day, six days a week, in a candy factory; she learned that little boys pulled basting threads out of garments sewn by their mothers, who worked for about ten cents an hour. Jane Addams was outraged and inaugurated a campaign for factory inspection and an eight-hour day for women. The first effort was successful but only temporarily, so the struggle went on.

During these years of work and strife, the experiment at Hull House was a success, and Jane Addams became famous in America. In an era when there were no social workers she was a pioneer and was called upon to speak to ever-larger audiences, and she published extensively. As her fame increased, her sphere of action broadened until it came to include an active attempt to put an end to war, and to inaugurate throughout the world a climate similar to Hull House where men and women of all nationalities met and mingled in friendship and peace.

At the turn of the twentieth century, because there were currents in motion that could lead to a major war, several peace congresses were held in the United States—congresses devoted to the ideal of perpetuating peace. Jane Addams was one of the leaders of these activities. The "practical idealist," she allowed herself to believe there really might be peace in the world. Unfortunately, in 1914 war was declared.

In 1915 a Women's Peace Party was organized in the United States and Jane Addams was made president. In the same year a call went out from the leading women of Europe for a congress to meet at The Hague to consider what could be done to end the war. As a representative of the most powerful neutral country and as president of the Women's Peace Party in the United States, Jane Addams was asked to preside. Henceforth she was not only Jane Addams of Hull House, but Jane Addams of the Women's International League for Peace and Freedom.

Regrettably, the League for Peace and Freedom did not achieve its aims. The women met at The Hague, resolutions were passed, delegates were sent to the warring countries asking for statements of intent and it was all futile. The statesmen insisted on "victory."

When Jane Addams returned to the United States, she was riding a tide of popularity. America stood for peace in a warring world, and so did she. Then, slowly, America slipped into the war, and with its increasing involvement came a change in public opinion. Jane Addams' ideals came to be suspect in the minds of many, and when she did not conform to the changing mood, her followers fell away. The country, in the throes of war, did not tolerate dissent. Because she opposed American involvement, the draft and the persecution of aliens, Jane Addams was branded a traitor; she was even denied the right to speak on some public platforms.

In the middle of 1918, the League for Peace and Freedom met again, in Zurich, Switzerland. At this congress, the delegates called for a League of Nations, based on Wilson's Fourteen Points, for women's voting rights and for the feeding of the starving millions of Europe, including the Germans.

Jane Addams' return home this time was in marked contrast to the popular reception she had received in 1915. When she attempted to appeal for food for the children of Europe, including those of Germany, she was accused of being pro-German, was trailed by detectives and was even suspected of being engaged in espionage!

Her work at Hull House went on, as did her work with the League of Peace and Freedom. Six times she presided over meetings of the league. Finally, in 1929, after a tenure of fourteen years, she forced through her resignation as president. In 1931, she and Nicholas Murray Butler were jointly awarded the Nobel Prize for Peace. She immediately turned her share over to the League for Peace and Freedom.

Jane Addams died on May 21, 1935. During the preceding decade, the mood of the country had changed to such an extent that she had again become one of its most honored citizens. Indicative of that change were the words written at the time of her death: "Her life was dedicated to a selfless service which has few parallels in the history of humanity; no person ever scaled higher peaks. . . ."

Nicholas Murray Butler
Peace Through Internationalism

1862–1947

The world into which Nicholas Murray Butler was born on April 2, 1862, in Elizabeth, New Jersey, was not a peaceful one. The United States was locked in a devastating civil war.

A precocious youth, Nicholas completed the first eight years of school in five, and before his eleventh birthday transferred into high school. Upon graduation, he was third in a class of thirteen.

When he entered Columbia, Butler intended to study law. But, in his junior year, the president of the college suggested that he seriously consider entering the field of education. Accepting the advice, Butler devoted himself to philosophy and education.

In 1884 he was awarded a Ph.D. That same year he sailed for Europe. After touring northern Europe, Butler settled down to study at the University of Berlin. Before he left home, many of Butler's professors gave him letters of introduction, which afforded him an opportunity to study under acknowledged masters.

Returning to New York in the fall of 1885, Butler accepted a position as assistant professor in philosophy at Columbia. It was the beginning of a meteoric rise in the academic world. In 1886, because his old philosophy professor was gravely ill, Butler became acting head of the Department of Philosophy. By 1889 he was its permanent head, and in 1890 when the Faculty of Philosophy was organized, he was made dean.

Contributing to Butler's increasing reputation as a pedagogue was his pioneering work in the establishment of Teachers College, later a part of Columbia University. This was one of the first centers for teacher training in the United States. Although still in his early thirties, Butler was offered the presidency of the new institution.

Despite his dual roles as president of Teachers College and dean at Columbia, Butler found time to accept a large number of invitations to speak on political or educational subjects. These speaking engagements carried him into every state of the Union and his name became well-known in the academic world.

In 1901, his achievements led the board of trustees to ask Butler to be president of Columbia University, a post that he accepted.

While primarily an administrator and academician, Butler could have entered politics on several occasions. A conservative, opposed to most major reforms, he became a power in the Republican party. A variety of offers to serve in a political capacity were offered him and all were refused. Butler preferred the role of critic and advisor.

Born into a society torn apart by the agony of civil war, Butler became an ardent advocate of the principles of arbitration and conciliation as methods of settling disputes. He developed the conviction in his student days that education was a primary condition for international cooperation; education not in the narrow sense of concentration in an academic discipline, but the kind of education that would develop an "international mind." He aligned himself with any movement contributing to that end, and on a number of occasions used the lecture platform to expound the cause of internationalism.

In connection with the work of the First Hague Conference, Butler, as a delegate of the United States, met and became friends with Paul d'Estournelles de Constant. Because of his long experience and his intimate understanding of European affairs, d'Estournelles became Butler's adviser and a partner in a periodical entitled *International Conciliation.* An organization bearing the same name was founded in 1905 and Butler became president of the American branch. Until the outbreak of war in 1914, he continued his involvement in any activity tending to promote international understanding.

In 1921, vitally concerned about the arms race between the victorious powers, Butler suggested to President-elect Warren Harding the idea of a disarmament conference to be held in Washington. Harding was agreeable; invitations were extended by the American State Department, and the Disarmament Conference was held in 1921-1922. It was moderately successful, and tension between the great powers, particularly over the building of warships, was diminished.

Vacationing in Europe in the summer of 1926, Butler spent a few weeks in Paris. While there he called on the French foreign minister, Aristide Briand. The Locarno Pact had just been signed, and Butler suggested to Briand it was time nations gave up war as an instrument of national policy and substituted peace.

Briand agreed; then he and others proposed that France and the United States sign a treaty embracing this concept, and Butler undertook to arouse public support. The result was the Kellogg-Briand Pact.

Nicholas Murray Butler deserves great credit for the pact. It was his suggestion to Briand that led to Briand's appeal, and it was his activities in America that led to its acceptance.

In 1931, as a reward for his manifold activities in the cause of peace, particularly the Kellogg-Briand Pact, Butler was chosen to share the Prize with Jane Addams. He was to live through another horrible war, but after 1932 he largely withdrew from all involvement in domestic and international affairs. He died in his home in New York on December 7, 1947.

Sir Ralph Norman Angell Lane
Peace Through the Pen

1874–1967

RALPH NORMAN ANGELL LANE, the thirty-sixth winner of
the Nobel Prize for Peace, was born into a well-to-do merchant's
family on December 26, 1874, in Holbeach, England. Norman's
father, who had begun life as a penniless apprentice in a department store, had forged ahead rapidly and eventually owned several stores of his own. Satisfied with the modest prosperity he had
achieved and more interested in books than business, he retired at
an early age.

Norman's future seemed to lie smoothly before him. But
something happened. In later years he believed the change in him

came in grammar school, when he was unjustly accused of lying in connection with a scandal involving a master and matron. No one at school spoke to him for a month and he began to question the world in which he lived.

Norman was sent away to a school in France when he was twelve. He found himself surrounded by two hundred boys, not one of whom spoke a word of English! Since he didn't speak French, he was lonely and lacked the consolation of books, which were available only in French. Then quite by accident someone dug up a copy of John Stuart Mill's *On Liberty* in English. Reading it, Norman was caught up in a tide of intellectual excitement; it challenged many of the assumptions that he had previously taken for granted; and it laid the foundation for his subsequent investigation of the intellectual life of Europe.

He did learn to read and write French fluently, but he was restless and bored, and so he returned to England. When he was fifteen, he found a position on a country weekly. The job lasted six months, and then he was engaged to edit a biweekly English paper in Geneva, Switzerland.

He accepted the position in Geneva so that he could attend lectures at the University of Geneva and could also consort with Russians and other revolutionaries who had congregated in the freest country in Europe.

The paper for which he worked had been established in Geneva to fit the needs of English tourists and to keep the permanent English colony in Switzerland informed about their own activities. Unfortunately, Norman had little interest in that kind of news. He was a young radical and he regarded the columns of the paper as a vehicle for his radical views. Finally Norman resigned and returned to England.

He found another position editing an evening paper published in Ipswich. Unchastened by his previous experience, he could not forego the pleasure of enlightening his readers; he would educate them whether they wanted it or not. Norman was asked to edit or resign. Convinced that newspaper owners were narrow-minded, he resigned.

Then Norman decided to emigrate to the United States. His wanderings came to an end in California where he worked as a ranch hand for over a year, then purchased a homestead from a settler and filed a claim. It was a difficult life at best. His homestead was in an area where running water was scarce, where the temperature soared in summer and it was bleakly cold in winter. But, in spite of the hardships, Norman was fairly happy. Then disaster struck. His claim was disallowed, and at the end of five years he was broke and had no future.

Fortunately, he did have his trade as a newspaperman. After working for a while in San Francisco, he drifted to St. Louis and then to Chicago, and finally, after seven years in the United States, he returned to England.

In 1898 Norman joined the *Daily Messenger*, an almost defunct newspaper in Paris. Soon made editor, he wrote a daily column on the Dreyfus case, then agitating the political world of France, and struggled to save the *Messenger* from going under. It failed and Norman was jobless.

While in America, Norman had steadfastly opposed America's policies toward Spain. Later he had opposed England's policies in South Africa which resulted in the Boer War and he condemned the French Government's role in the Dreyfus case. In 1902-03 he compiled his experiences into a book published under the title *Patriotism Under Three Flags: A Plea for Rationalism in Politics*. His major theme was how human judgment is warped and changed by an emotionalism that draws its strength from irrational sources an individual may not even be aware of.

Norman found a new position, the best he was ever to hold in the world of journalism, as publisher of the Paris edition of the London *Daily Mail*. He was given complete responsibility for the paper, as well as complete editorial freedom. No attempt was made to supervise what he printed and, on several occasions, his Paris *Daily Mail* contradicted the London *Daily Mail*.

Norman's job lasted ten years. The paper he edited continued to grow in circulation, but by 1912 he was so much in demand as a speaker that he found lecture dates interfering with his work. His popularity stemmed from the publication of a book which took the Continent by storm: *The Great Illusion*. He published the book under the pen name Norman Angell and used that name from then on.

While few in Europe or England seriously entertained the possibility of war, tensions had risen due to the arms race taking place and Europe becoming divided into two armed camps. Angell suggested in his book that men in each camp come to some conclusions as to what they wanted and then sit down and rationally discuss how those wants could be met; he further suggested that war had never been and could never be anything but economic disaster for those involved. The response to the book was overwhelming.

For the next several years, Angell enthusiastically dedicated himself to the prevention of the outbreak of war. In speeches, in pamphlets, in personal meetings with leading statesmen, Angell emphasized again and again that "war is not the outcome of fate, or nature, or the inevitable process of history. It is not made by nature but by men; it represents the failure of human wisdom." And he argued that wisdom need not fail. The nations seated around a conference table, he believed, could work out ways to achieve their ends without resort to war.

But Angell was no utopian dreamer. His book *Patriotism Under Three Flags* demonstrated that he was aware the irrational element in public opinion could drive statesmen further than they wished to go. Hence he worked desperately in the years before the war to mold public opinion.

He was not without help, either moral or financial. The Carnegie Endowment arranged for an advertising campaign in Germany for his book, *The Great Illusion*, and it sponsored a series of lectures by him. Norman Angell clubs spread across the world, but human wisdom did fail, and the Western nations plunged into the maelstrom of war.

When the war ended and the League of Nations was established, Angell became one of its most ardent advocates.

In the early 1920's Angell joined the Labor party, believing it was more internationally minded than the Conservative party. In 1929 he won a seat in Parliament but soon became convinced he had made a mistake. His cause was peace, and as an active politician, he had to spend too much time dealing with trivial matters in which he had no interest. He retired in 1931 to again devote himself to League affairs.

The year he retired from Parliament he was knighted, becoming Sir Norman Angell. Two years later he was awarded the Nobel Prize for Peace. Angell found it somewhat ironic that he received fewer telegrams congratulating him upon winning the Peace Prize than when he was knighted. Apparently people were more interested in such trivia as knighthood than in a man's work for peace.

During the 1930's, Angell worked desperately and despairingly for his principle of collective security as the only sure method of averting another war. But the old panacea for the establishment of world peace, the League of Nations, failed. Why? For Angell the answer was simple. The League failed not because of implicit defects, although it had many, but because world opinion, which ultimately must govern the action of nations, had not been educated to intelligently evaluate means and ends.

After the fall of France in 1940, although in his late sixties and in ill health, Angell made a lecture tour of the United States. He was convinced that the only hope for the democracies in World War II was the intervention of America. This was his last major effort for the cause in which he believed. Following the war, he drifted into retirement and died on October 25, 1967, in Croydon, England. He was ninety-two years old.

Arthur Henderson
Peace Through Disarmament

1863–1935

ARTHUR HENDERSON was born on September 13, 1863, in Glasgow, Scotland. His family was constantly on the verge of economic disaster. There was rarely enough food in the house; clothes were scanty and ragged; ill health was a catastrophe. When Arthur was nine, his father became sick and died.

Shortly after his father's death, his mother remarried and the family moved to Newcastle-Upon-Tyne. There, at the age of twelve, Arthur was forced to find work.

He became an apprentice iron molder at the Locomotive and General Foundry Works, a huge, worldwide firm. He completed his apprenticeship at the ironworks at seventeen, then found a position as a journeyman iron founder in Southampton.

In the 1880's unions weren't exactly illegal, but if a worker joined a union he was a marked man—the first to be laid off, the last to be hired. Nevertheless, aware of the problems the workers faced and of the need for organization, Henderson joined the Friendly Society of Ironworkers in Southampton.

Returning to Newcastle-Upon-Tyne, Henderson found work again at the foundry. Intelligent and possessing the kind of personality people find attractive, within a year of his return to Newcastle, he became the unpaid secretary of the local lodge of the Ironworkers Society and, as such, a man considered dangerous by the managers of the locomotive works. Every year thereafter while he was employed by the foundry, Henderson could count upon being laid off from work for a number of months. There were, however, some compensations for his lack of employment; he became an authority on union matters, admired and respected by union men.

In the following years, Henderson involved himself in a variety of positions—appointive and elective—that brought him to the forefront of the labor movement in England. He served as a town councillor of Newcastle, and was elected a member of the Durham County Council. In 1899, he attended the historic London conference of socialists and trade unionists which set up the Labor Representation Committee—the foundation of the Labor party. In 1903, he was made mayor of the Darlington Borough Council, secretary of the Labor Representation Committee, coauthored a book with Ramsay MacDonald, and was elected to Parliament as a Labor candidate.

Henderson entered Parliament as one of five Labor MP's who were affiliated with neither the Liberals nor the Conservatives. None of the Labor MP's could exercise much power. The best they could do was vote as benefited the cause of labor and work to build up the Labor party, which was formally brought into being during a conference presided over by Henderson in 1906.

In Parliament, as the Labor MP's increased in numbers, Henderson appeared as the chief figure in making the Labor members a cohesive and effective group. Officially parliamentary leader of the party between 1908-1911, Henderson, a modest man, promoted Ramsay MacDonald to party leadership in 1911, and contented himself with becoming party secretary, a post he was to hold for the next twenty-three years.

Henderson was originally opposed to World War I. But when Germany invaded Belgium, he changed his mind. This act of aggression, to him, justified breaking the weak ties binding German and British labor; it justified war.

Convinced of the validity of England's cause, Henderson became a wholehearted participant in the drive toward victory. In late 1914, he succeeded Ramsay MacDonald as leader of the Labor party when MacDonald resigned rather than support the war, and a year later he became a member of Herbert Asquith's coalition, the first Laborite to gain Cabinet rank.

After the war, Henderson threw himself into the building up of the Labor party and to such good effect that in 1924 the Conservatives were overthrown. Ramsay MacDonald then formed the first Labor Government in English history and Henderson became Home Secretary. However, in the fall of 1924, MacDonald made the mistake of calling for a general election and the Laborites were badly defeated. It took five years to reorganize the party, and in May of 1929 the Laborites came back into power. This time, as the principle architect of Labor's victory, Henderson was put in charge of the Foreign Office.

While never quite attaining first rank, Henderson was a good Foreign Secretary. Working closely with Aristide Briand of France and Gustav Stresemann of Germany, he did much to help establish amicable relations between the three countries. In 1931, his reputation as a sincere advocate of peace having become worldwide, he was nominated by Briand and unanimously chosen by the Council of the League to serve as chairman of the International Disarmament Conference to meet in 1932.

The Disarmament Conference, the culmination of all of Henderson's hopes, was a logical final step to world peace. But it was a fiasco. Preoccupied with economics due to the world depression that began in 1929, the nations refused to take disarmament seriously.

Henderson was aware of what was at stake. In his opening address he announced, "I refuse to contemplate even the possibility of failure; but if we fail, no one can foretell the evil consequences that might ensue."

During the first session, Henderson was too ill to serve as chairman. He was in better health when the second session met in 1933 and some progress was achieved; then Germany withdrew from the conference and that was really the end.

In December of 1934, the Nobel Committee awarded the Peace Prize to Henderson for his work at the Disarmament Conference. In keeping with tradition, he was invited to deliver a lecture before the Nobel Committee and the Storting. Honored by the award and viewing the lecture as another opportunity to plead his cause, Henderson accepted. In ringing tones, Henderson reaffirmed his belief that:

> There is no greater human issue upon which hope concentrates than the cause of disarmament. There is no greater achievement to be realized than that of securing the world's peace. There is no greater action in the world than that of leading the people to peace, freedom and security.

Henderson still struggled to keep the conference alive. Ill, overly tired and in constant pain, he carried on until 1935. Finally, in his seventy-second year, the operation postponed too often was performed. He survived it, and for a time appeared to rally; then he slowly grew weaker and died in London on October 20, 1935.

Carl von Ossietzky
Martyr for his Cause

1889–1938

Unlike many of the men who have won a Nobel Prize for Peace, Carl von Ossietzky was never a great leader. He lived as an obscure journalist and editor whom fame touched a moment before his death. But he deserved the Prize he won.

Ossietzky was born on October 3, 1889, in Hamburg, Germany, a large industrial town some hundreds of miles north of Braunau-am-Inn, in Austria, where Adolph Hitler—whose strange and twisted path was to cross Ossietzky's—had been born on April 20th. His father was a poor but respectable merchant, so well-loved that his friends offered to raise money to send his intelligent son to a university. The boy refused to go. He was interested in becoming a writer, and by the time he was twenty he had published poetry in a Munich periodical.

Early in life, Carl became a confirmed opponent of war and was sure the developing German militarism was leading in that direction. He feared that the military had become the "arbiters of destiny and rulers of the state" and that all aspects of German life had been subordinated to a clique dedicated to destruction.

In 1912, Ossietzky took an active part in the founding of the Hamburg branch of the German Peace Society. But the tocsins of war were already sounding in Germany, as in all the nations of Western Europe.

Ossietzky was a pacifist, but he was a German citizen, subject to German law. When war broke out he was immediately drafted, and spent 1914 to 1918 in the trenches of eastern France.

Upon his discharge, Ossietzky went to Berlin. Convinced before the war of its futility, now certain of its horror, he was intent upon using every resource at his command to ensure the preservation of peace. He edited and wrote for several magazines and served briefly as the secretary of the German Peace Society.

In the early 1920's, Ossietzky helped publish a series of articles calling attention to outrages being committed by right-wing terrorist societies. The terrorists were supported by the Army, which struck back at Ossietzky. Writs of libel were issued against him and he was tried and fined.

A man with less courage, or less hatred of the military, might have refrained from publishing articles attacking the Army after the trial and conviction. It was obvious that if he persisted he would, sooner or later, be sent to prison. But Ossietzky was adamant. He was arrested again but released.

Finally, in 1924, Ossietzky joined the staff of the magazine *Die Weltbühne* (*World State*) as coeditor. He became editor in 1927. In 1929 he published an article by Walter Kreiser entitled "Queer Happenings in German Aviation," which argued that the Ministry of Transport was using commercial flying as a screen for military rearmament. The charge was true, but the truth of the matter was irrelevant. Both Ossietzky and Kreiser were arrested for revealing military secrets.

Intent only upon silencing Ossietzky, the Government did not immediately bring him to trial or even bar him from publishing. It waited to see if he had learned his lesson. He had not. He published articles attempting to unite the people against Hitler and National Socialism and, early in 1931, he wrote a spirited defense of a film unpopular with the Government entitled *All Quiet on the Western Front.*

It was an act of defiance and the Government brought him to a secret trial. In November, 1931, he was sentenced to prison. Even then he need not have gone to jail; friends advised him to flee. But Ossietzky refused. Flight, he said, "leaves man a hollow voice in which to speak to his countrymen." He warned other journalists against the danger of not speaking out against secret trials, of being silent in the face of injustice. Then in May, 1932, he gave himself up to the authorities.

After serving seven months, he was released when the Government declared a Christmas amnesty for political prisoners. Again friends urged him to get out of Germany, and again he refused.

In January, 1933, Hitler was made head of the German state. The opponents of Nazism could expect no mercy; they received none. On February 27, 1933, Ossietzky was arrested again. There was no examination, no trial, nothing. He was an enemy of the state, doomed to spend the remainder of his life in concentration camps.

The Nazis could force him to be silent. They could not, however, obliterate his name or the memory of his courageous stand for truth and justice. As early as 1934, the Nobel Committee began to receive petitions asking that Ossietzky be considered for the Peace Prize. One petition stated ". . . we say that he has done more than any of us, and we believe that he has done most of all living men to deserve this acknowledgment from his fellowmen."

The Nazis were aware that Ossietzky was a candidate for the Prize and the Nobel Committee was warned that it must not provoke the German people by rewarding a "traitor to our nation." But in 1935, in defiance of Hitler and all he stood for, the award went to Carl von Ossietzky.

Hitler issued a decree forbidding any German to accept a Nobel Prize. But aware of the fame now attached to Ossietzky's name, the Nazis transferred him from prison camp to a hospital. He was suffering from a bad heart and tuberculosis, and in 1935 the Nazis were still somewhat concerned about appearances; it wouldn't do to have a Nobel Prize winner in a concentration camp.

He was even allowed to be interviewed—under close supervision—by Berlin correspondents. There was little that he could say. He did suggest that he would be glad to go to Oslo to receive the award, and he even promised not to say anything that would cause trouble between Germany and Norway. But the Government would not permit it and, in any case, he was far too sick to make the trip.

Ossietzky was allowed to read the immense flood of letters and telegrams congratulating him, but the German government took a large portion of the Prize money as compensation for his board and lodging while he was in prisons and concentration camps; his lawyer stole the rest.

In the spring of 1938, Ossietzky died from tuberculosis, a victim of the evil the world had allowed to engulf Germany.

Carlos Saavedra Lamas
Peacemaker in the Bolivia-Paraguay Chaco War

1878–1959

In December, 1936, Carlos Saavedra Lamas, the only Latin American to be so honored, was awarded the Nobel Prize for Peace. Although the bestowal of the Prize had often been questioned, never before had there been such a controversial candidate. For years, seemingly with no qualms of conscience, Saavedra Lamas had served a dictator; and in 1935 he had accepted the Iron Cross from Hitler. Yet a study of Saavedra Lamas' life indicates that the Committee did have reason to make their choice.

Saavedra Lamas was born to position and wealth in Buenos Aires on November 1, 1878. His education was directed initially by private tutors. In his early teens, he was sent to the best private school available. A brilliant student, he graduated with honors and went abroad for further study.

By the time he returned to Buenos Aires, Saavedra Lamas had decided to become a lawyer. But after graduating *summa cum laude* from the University of Buenos Aires, in 1903, he accepted a position as professor of international law at the University Law School and settled down to a career of teaching and writing.

In 1906, he was called upon to become the Director of Public Credit, and a year later Secretary of the Municipality of Buenos Aires. Then he became a national deputy and, in 1915, he was appointed Minister of Justice and Public Education.

With excellent connections in the ruling class, Saavedra Lamas' future in politics could have developed into whatever he wanted it to be. However, he was not overly interested in elective offices. He made little effort to involve himself in politics and his service as Minister of Justice and Public Education lasted only a brief time.

In the years following, Saavedra Lamas gained an enormous reputation as a jurist in both his native country and internationally. As a result, in 1927, he was appointed a delegate to the Jurists Convention held in Rio de Janeiro, and the following year he was elected president of the International Labor Conference held in Geneva. Then, in 1932, he was appointed Foreign Minister.

Once in the Foreign Office, Saavedra Lamas moved swiftly to establish Argentina's place in the community of nations. He published a proposed antiwar treaty similar to the Kellogg-Briand Pact. Then he journeyed to Montevideo to participate in the deliberations of the Seventh Pan-American Conference in December of 1933.

At the Conference, American Secretary of State, Cordell Hull, intent upon furthering Franklin D. Roosevelt's "Good Neighbor Policy" and aware that the cooperation of Argentina was vitally necessary, paid assiduous court to Saavedra Lamas, eagerly supported his antiwar pact and encouraged him in his efforts to end the Chaco War between Paraguay and Bolivia.

Initially, when trouble developed between Paraguay and Bolivia, a commission of "neutrals" had been set up to seek a solution. The commission proved ineffective and, when he became Foreign Minister, Saavedra Lamas was instrumental in liquidating its efforts. Then he blocked settlement of the dispute by a League of Nations commission and had the affair entrusted to a commission composed of representatives from neighboring states. As the Foreign Minister of the most powerful state in Latin America, he was able to play the leading role in arriving at a solution to the dispute. Thus, when a truce was finally signed in 1935, Saavedra Lamas received the credit and was awarded the Peace Prize in 1936. It was a simple case of giving the Prize to a man who had been instrumental in stopping a war, the same reason the Prize had been awarded to Theodore Roosevelt in 1906.

The Nobel award had been preceded by another honor in 1936, when Saavedra Lamas was elected president of the Assembly of the League of Nations. But world renown did not keep him in office. In 1938 Augustin Justo, who had been a ruthless dictator, retired and Saavedra Lamas followed him into private life.

Returning to the University of Buenos Aires, Lamas again taught international law and between 1941 and 1943 served as the university's president. Finally, in 1946, he retired. Twelve years later, in 1958, he suffered a brain hemorrhage and, on May 5, 1959, he died.

Viscount Cecil of Chelwood
Laborer for the League

1864–1958

LORD CECIL of Chelwood was born Edgar Algernon Robert Cecil in London on September 14, 1864. His father was one of England's important political figures, and Robert grew up in a household of wealth and leisure.

In 1877, when he was thirteen, Robert was sent to Eton and, in the fall of 1882, he matriculated at Oxford.

He found the university strikingly different from secondary school. In the 1880's, it was comparatively easy to get through Oxford without overextending oneself intellectually, but there were serious students on the campus. Cecil reveled in the discussions, and the long, serious, talks in his "diggings" or rooms. His greatest joy, however, was the "union," the center for political debate on campus. Here the serious student, the brilliant or the witty had opportunity to exercise his talents.

In 1886, having decided to become a lawyer, Edgar Algernon Robert Cecil went to London in search of fame and fortune. Fortune he won, rather swiftly; but fame eluded his grasp for a number of years. In 1894 he had qualified for practice by passing the stringent law examinations and he was established in his own chambers.

Still a young man, with a position at the bar and a good practice, Cecil was free to consider a political career. In 1905 he ran for election to Parliament and was successful. But the year of his election saw his party, the Conservative party, overwhelmingly defeated at the polls. Thus, he found himself a member of the Opposition.

In one respect the defeat of the Conservatives had beneficial results for Cecil. With many of the leading men of his party defeated he made a name for himself as one of the most vociferous critics of the Government.

When war came in 1914, Cecil was fifty years old—too old for active service. Instead he joined the Red Cross and took over the responsibility of organizing the Department of the Wounded and Missing in Paris. It was a depressing task. Poring over lists of the dead, wounded and missing, inspecting the hospitals in Paris, talking to young men dying from a mustard gas attack, Cecil learned at first hand the barbarism of war, and conceived an implacable hatred for it.

In the summer of 1915, Cecil was called home from Paris to become Under Secretary for Foreign Affairs. He was immediately assigned a difficult and delicate task. He was made responsible for the establishment and maintenance of the British blockade of Europe.

During the last years of the war, Cecil's overriding interest, aside from winning the war, came to focus upon the prospects of a League of Nations. He felt that all nations should exert every effort to avoid modern warfare. As early as 1916, when the outcome of the war was still very much in doubt, he suggested that a committee be appointed to draw up a draft of a League Covenant —or agreement—to be signed by the various nations. Such a committee was appointed and its work constituted the first attempt under government auspices to come to grips with the problem of establishing principles for a world organization.

On February 14, 1919, in Paris, Woodrow Wilson presented the proposed Covenant of the League of Nations to the Peace Conference. When he finished, Cecil, as the British representative, was next to speak. After touching upon the major provisions of the Covenant, he closed by remarking that the drafting committee "didn't want to produce a finished building, but only to lay a solid foundation on which one could be built." He was quite right, the building was not finished. And his hope that, once established, the League's weaknesses and faults could be rectified by appropriate legislation was not to happen.

Returning to England, Cecil was elected chairman of the League of Nations Union, and the affairs of the League of Nations engrossed all his energy for the next two decades. In 1920, he attended the first assembly of the League as a representative of South Africa. In 1921, again as a representative of South Africa, he presented a report to the Committee of the Secretariat dealing with disarmament, and subsequently became a member of the Disarmament Section of the Secretariat. In 1922, he represented South Africa at the third assembly meeting of the League.

Constantly working on behalf of the League or on its affairs and being one of the guiding hands in League deliberations, eventually took its toll on a man over sixty years old. In 1927, in Geneva, Cecil suffered a nervous breakdown from overwork. He paid little attention to nature's danger signal and was soon working harder than ever.

In 1937, Cecil was awarded the Nobel Prize for Peace for his work with the League of Nations. But he and the others who shared his labors failed in their mission despite their arduous work.

It was, however, no personal failure. As he himself phrased it in 1940, there will never be peace:

> Unless the nations genuinely accept the view that peace is the greatest of national interests and are consequently ready to maintain with all their strength a Peace approved by international authority as being founded on Freedom, Truth and Justice.

By that time another war had come; when it ended, Cecil was eighty-one, far too old to engage in peace movements or organizations. He died on November 24, 1958.

Cordell Hull
Father of the United Nations

1871–1955

CORDELL HULL was born October 2, 1871, on a plateau farm in Tennessee. Among mountain families in those days, usually only one son, if any, was chosen to get a higher education. Determined to become a lawyer, Cordell was faced with the necessity of convincing his father that he was the one who ought to be educated. When he was fourteen, he proved his case by winning a debating contest.

At the Montvale Academy in Celina, Tenn., Cordell rapidly emerged as the star pupil in his class. He was so capable that his teacher urged him to go on to college before settling down to study law. He transferred to the Normal School at Bowling Green, Kentucky, for a term. Then he spent a year at the National Normal University at Lebanon, Ohio. Finally he returned to Celina and began to study law. He was so determined to succeed that, in 1891, although not yet twenty-one, he took the state bar examination and passed with flying colors.

One might think that, having worked so hard to become a lawyer, Hull would have settled down to building up a clientele. But his studies had created in him a greater concern for public rather than private affairs, so he decided to run for the state legislature.

His only political experience was as a county delegate to the State Democratic Convention. But he was obviously sincere and honest and had facts to support his arguments. The voters were impressed and in 1892, Hull won his first election.

At the end of his second term, he refused to run again, and returned to Celina. A vacancy occurred among the circuit judges, and the governor appointed Hull to fill the vacancy. Hardly three years of his second term as judge had expired before he submitted his resignation in order to run for the United States House of Representatives. He was elected and, in 1907, took his seat in the newly convened Sixtieth Congress.

In the House, Hull turned out to be the very antithesis of the frock-coated, eloquent, flamboyant southern politician. Quiet, rarely speaking on the floor, he preferred to achieve his ends through committee work and private conferences. He became an expert on such complex issues as tariff revision and taxes, and was the author of the federal income tax law of 1913.

When the United States declared war in 1917, Hull turned his attention to the causes of wars and what could be done about them. He came to the conclusion that one cause of war was tariff barriers, and he tried to persuade his colleagues in the House either to abolish tariffs altogether or to arrive at them by international agreement. Unfortunately, he failed, largely because of the overwhelming defeat of the Democratic party at the polls in 1920. Hull himself was defeated for reelection.

However, he was reelected in 1922, and by the end of the 1920's he had gained a reputation as one of the most important congressmen in Washington. Then, in 1931, he won election to the Senate. But his stay there was brief. In January of 1933, President-elect Franklin D. Roosevelt offered him the position of Secretary of State.

As Secretary of State, Hull began to work on a reciprocal trade program. He and the President believed reciprocal trade agreements would not only revive trade, but would help build up international prosperity and help American agriculture to find world markets.

As important as trade agreements was the new departure in foreign policy vis-à-vis Latin America, and, in 1933, President Roosevelt laid down the foundation of the "Good Neighbor Policy." Emphasizing the necessity of increasing trade and commerce among the nations of the Western Hemisphere, the administration also showed interest in a policy of nonintervention.

The Seventh Pan-American Conference held in Montevideo, Uruguay in December, 1933, gave the American Government an opportunity to demonstrate that it meant what it said. Hull's conduct at the Conference served to underscore the new shift in American diplomacy, and in a speech delivered at the closing session, he pledged the United States to a policy of nonintervention in Latin America.

All in all, the conference was a success. Hull's modesty, his refusal to exploit the power of the United States, his willingness to negotiate, did much to eradicate the fears and suspicions with which most Latin Americans regarded the United States.

Back in Washington, Hull set about expediting the pledge of nonintervention in Latin America. In 1934, American troops were withdrawn from Haiti and the Platt Amendment with Cuba, in force since 1903, was abrogated. These actions generated a new surge of confidence in the United States, no longer regarded as the bully of the North, but as a friend.

Thanks to the work Hull had done at Montevideo, the Conference for the Maintenance of Peace in Buenos Aires in 1936 further strengthened the "Good Neighbor Policy." It was agreed that if the peace of the Americas were challenged, the republics would meet to find a cooperative solution. Approval was given to the proposal that the republics would remain neutral in any war outside of the hemisphere or between two nations within. Finally, it was agreed that all differences between the nations must be submitted to arbitration. These summed up to a sweeping change in United States-Latin American relations: the historic Monroe Doctrine had become multilateral.

In 1939 war began in Europe. Hull was aware that trouble was also brewing in the Pacific. But he wanted peace and believed even late in 1941 that it might be possible.

However, a series of meetings between Hull and Japanese representatives, and an exchange of proposals and counterproposals, proved fruitless. On the afternoon of December 7, 1941, the Japanese envoys met with Hull and informed him that their Government flatly rejected the latest American terms. That morning, even before the meeting took place, Japanese planes had bombed Pearl Harbor. The United States was again at war. But out of this war was to come a new hope.

It is difficult to trace the origin of the United Nations; it was a dream that existed in the minds of many men. Its organizational development probably began as early as August, 1941, when Franklin D. Roosevelt and Winston Churchill met and agreed on what came to be known as the Atlantic Charter. The seed planted then grew slowly until finally, at Yalta, in February, 1945, Roosevelt, Churchill and Joseph Stalin agreed that the United Nations should be established as soon as possible.

From the beginning of the war, Hull had worked indefatigably for the establishment of such an organization. In every conference of the foreign ministers he had pushed and prodded, argued and fought, sometimes meeting objections or answering questions, other times utilizing the prestige of the United States to gain a point. Fertile in imagination and argument, dedicated to his cause, he became known, in the words of President Roosevelt, as the "Father of the UN."

He did not attend the conference at San Francisco where the world organization was established. Suffering badly from diabetes and arteriosclerosis, exhausted from his years of labor in the State Department, he resigned in November, 1944. A year later, in recognition for his work in promoting peace in the Western Hemisphere, for attempting to avert war in the world through international trade agreements, and for his work in establishing the United Nations, he was awarded the Nobel Prize for Peace.

He was seventy-four the year of the award and very ill. Every time he entered the United States Naval Hospital at Bethesda, Maryland, during the next ten years, friends expected it to be the last; but every time he would recover. Finally, on July 24, 1955, he sank into a coma and died.

Emily Greene Balch
A Woman's Search for Peace

1867–1961

EMILY GREENE BALCH was born into the home of a well-to-do Boston lawyer on January 8, 1867. After attending the best schools in Boston, in the fall of 1886 she went to Bryn Mawr to study classics; but in her senior year she also studied economics and became fascinated by it.

Graduating in 1889, at the top of her class, she was awarded the first European scholarship given to a Bryn Mawr student, and sailed for Europe in 1890 to continue her studies in political economy.

After a year at the Sorbonne, she returned to the United

States and became a staff member at Denison House. Denison House, like Hull House in Chicago, had been established to give aid and comfort to the poor in Boston and to help train them to meet the complexities of the modern industrial world. Emily might have pursued a career as a settlement house worker had she not discovered a fascinating vocation: teaching.

However, she thought she needed more education to teach college so she studied at the University of Chicago and at Radcliffe, then went to Europe again, this time to spend a year at the University of Berlin. A chance meeting led to the offer of a position at Wellesley. She accepted, and began an association with that school that was to last until 1918.

The young assistant professor in economics who took up her duties in the fall of 1896 had become one of the best educated women in the United States. Described by a student as "an utterly unpretentious woman, spare of figure, unmindful of clothes and fripperies," she radiated efficiency. In the years between 1896 and 1913 she moved up through the academic ranks to become a professor of economics and head of the Economics Department at Wellesley. She was also one of the founders of the Women's Trade Union League of America, a member of the Factory Inspection Commission in Massachusetts, chairman of the Massachusetts Minimum Wage Commission—she helped draft the first minimum wage law in the country— a member of the Massachusetts Commission on Immigration and wrote *Our Slavic Fellow-Citizens* (1910), which is still one of the most important studies of Slavic immigration to this country. An impressive record; but in 1913 she was on the threshold of the most important phase of her career, that of a leader in the international peace movement.

Emily shared the popular belief that there would never be another major war. The world, she thought, had become too civilized to spend its treasure to no end. She was wrong, but, when war did come she felt something had to be done to stop it, and so she joined a number of women in the Western world who were united in opposition to war. A call went out from various women's peace parties to meet at The Hague and, in 1915, Emily Balch, Jane Addams and some forty-five other women sailed for Holland to attend the first Women's Congress.

Delegates from fifteen neutral and belligerent nations met at The Hague for speeches and discussions, arguments and prayers, but nothing was accomplished to stop the war. The failure was not for lack of trying; and Emily Balch was one of those who tried the hardest. She was coauthor of a set of proposals that eventually led to the creation of the Women's International League for Peace and Freedom. She was sent by the Women's Congress on a delegation to Russia and the Scandinavian countries to urge neutral mediation and, in 1916, she spent several months in Stockholm working on the Neutral Conference for Continuous Mediation. Finally, in late 1916, she returned to the United States, her mission a failure.

She did not return to Wellesley. In late 1916, as the United States was slipping ever closer to intervention in the war, her conscience forced her to take some action. She joined the staff of *The Nation*, which was opposed to war, she helped found the American Union vs Militarism, she joined in peace parades, spoke at giant mass meetings and, in general, involved herself in what the *New York Evening Sun* described as, "doing the work of sedition and treachery."

Miss Balch had to pay for her stand on the war and her opinions about peace. In 1918, her five-year appointment at Wellesley came to an end and the trustees decided not to reappoint her. They claimed her antiwar efforts, her views on pacifism and economics had made her "notorious." She was not, therefore, the kind of person best fitted to teach the young ladies at Wellesley. Despite rigorous protests on her behalf by other members of the faculty and staff, the trustees dismissed her, and at fifty-one, her professional life brought to a close, she faced an uncertain future.

Then in 1919, she was chosen as a delegate to attend the Second Women's Congress and she stayed on as its international secretary-treasurer. That same year the Women's International

League for Peace and Freedom (WILPF) was founded in Geneva and Miss Balch became a member of its permanent staff.

For almost two decades Emily Blach was intimately associated with WILPF. From the League's headquarters in Geneva she helped organize conferences on drug control and disarmament; she represented WILPF on a committee of six to investigate conditions in Haiti during the American occupation; she published extensively and, in 1929, she was named to a three-member presidium to run WILPF, after Jane Addams resigned as president.

In 1931, with WILPF, Miss Balch successfully urged the award of the Peace Prize to Jane Addams. In 1935, in defiance of Hitler, she supported the awarding of the Prize to Carl von Ossietzky. She published extensively on problems of peace, attended congresses and meetings; and all to no apparent end.

In 1936, the year that she was named honorary international president of WILPF, Hitler marched into the Rhineland. The year she published *Refugees as Assets* (1939), Hitler invaded Poland and World War II began.

A pacifist who had fought to keep the United States out of World War I, Miss Balch was no pacifist when the Western world faced a death struggle with Hitler and Mussolini. She favored Roosevelt's Lend-Lease Act and regarded the strength of America the world's single hope to oppose the mechanized might of Germany and Japan. But she did not believe that the end of the war was to be "victory." The cessation of the fighting was merely a means to an end, the only true "victory" would be the peace of the world.

As the war drew to a close, she headed a committee of WILPF that urged a negotiated peace rather than unconditional surrender; and in the years after the war she became an ardent advocate of the United Nations.

In 1946, a group of men and women, including the famous American philosopher, John Dewey, proposed that Emily Balch be awarded the Nobel Prize for Peace. In December, the telegram arrived informing her she had been selected. She accepted the Prize in the name of WILPF which she had represented for so many years and, to continue its activities, she donated the bulk of the Prize money to it.

In 1946, Emily Balch was seventy-nine years old; obviously the years of intense activity were over. But in 1948, she went on a tour for the One World Committee, whose objective was to establish peaceful relations between the nations of the world. She continued to publish, urging support of the United Nations, and constantly warned the public of the dangers that develop when propagandists fan the flames of hatred between nations. Finally, in 1956, she grew too weak to do more than write a few letters to the editor of *The New York Times*. She moved into a nursing home, and, on January 10, 1961, she died at the age of ninety-four.

John R. Mott
To Ease War's Horrors

1865–1955

JOHN R. MOTT was born May 25, 1865, in Sullivan County, New York. Four months later, his family moved to Postville, Iowa. After establshing himself in the lumber business, John's father emerged as the most prosperous man in the community. In the late 1860's he was elected the town's first mayor.

Considering that John Mott was to win his great reputation in the church, it is interesting to note that he was not brought up in a religious atmosphere. The Mott children attended Sunday school and, while they were good Christians, John's parents were opposed to his going into church work.

When John was thirteen, a Quaker minister held a revival meeting in the village and Mott was converted. Later, the local Methodist minister stimulated and encouraged the boy's interest in both religion and education. The result was that when Mott finished high school, in the fall of 1881, he enrolled in Upper Iowa University at Fayette.

Mott proved so apt a student that his professor encouraged him to do advanced work in history and political science, and when he graduated from Upper Iowa, he was admitted to Cornell University in Ithaca, New York.

Upon his arrival at Cornell in the fall of 1885, Mott was met at the station by members of the University Christian Association who helped him to find rooms and called on him several times. John was touched by their helpfulness and consideration, and he joined the association. Less than a year later, in January, 1886, impressed by a speaker from the Young Men's Christian Association, Mott decided to dedicate his life to the service of Christ. That dedication was complete, sincere and lasting.

During his years at Cornell, Mott had offers that could have launched him on an academic career. He was tempted; a life of scholarship appealed to him. But early in 1888, he accepted a position traveling from college to college in the United States and Canada as a YMCA representative.

In 1891 Mott took his first trip abroad to attend a conference in Amsterdam of the World's Alliance of Young Men's Christian Associations.

Four years later, at a conference in Sweden, Mott put together the World Student Christian Federation. The federation was in no way a competitor of the YMCA. Rather, its activities supplemented and reenforced those of the older organization.

Mott's travels of over two million miles in the service of the federation and the YMCA included four trips around the world, visits to Africa, South America, Australia, New Zealand, Canada and every country in Europe, including Russia. He was also the editor of a magazine and the author of several books. Perhaps

Nathan Söderblom characterized Mott best in referring to him as "the Napoleon of the Christian student movement."

When war broke out in Europe in 1914, Mott and his associates fought valiantly to prevent the breakup of the organizations they had helped put together to carry forward the work of salvation. But with the young men of England, France, Germany and Austria killing each other, the possibility of saving the YMCAs was remote. There were, however, practical things to be done, on an impartial basis. The need was greatest among prisoners of war and the YMCA in America raised tens of millions of dollars to offer the prisoners opportunities for worship, and training in handicrafts, moving pictures, and educational and recreational facilities.

After the United States entered the war in 1917, American work among prisoners of war almost ceased, but there was much to be done among the millions of American troops. Because there were several organizations involved in raising money to help the soldiers, President Wilson asked Mott to become director of a unified campaign. He accepted, and demonstrated again his magnificent organizing ability. Starting with a goal of $170,000,000, the final sum raised was considerably over $200,000,000. As head of the YMCA (during the war, he became general secretary of the International Committee of the YMCA) and responsible for its many activities, Mott received the Distinguished Service Medal for welfare service rendered throughout the war.

Long before the war, as a man of God, Mott had been a devotee of peace and of the principle of arbitration, a cause he assiduously pursued throughout the 1920's and 1930's. In the YMCA and the other organizations he headed or to which he belonged, he always utilized the weight of his prestige and influence to oppose all forms of prejudice and social discrimination—factors which often contribute to war. In a multitude of conferences held throughout the world, he brought together students of all nations and of all races, where they met on a basis of absolute equality. Believing in the fatherhood of God, Mott could not but

166

believe in the brotherhood of man. Paradoxically, within the United States, Mott did little to end discrimination in the YMCAs of the South.

John Mott was seventy-four in 1939, when World War II broke out. But as in World War I, he immediately moved into action. Again vast sums of money were raised for the work of the YMCA, and again the "Y" tendered relief to prisoners of war, as it had since the Civil War.

When the war came to an end, Mott was old, and the days of travel and endless conferences were over. In 1946, he was awarded the Nobel Prize, with Emily Balch, in recognition of his work for peace and for humane treatment of prisoners of war and for the elimination of discrimination and prejudice from the world.

During the last ten years of his life, he lived in retirement in Orlando, Florida. He died on January 31, 1955, at the age of ninety.

Baron John Boyd-Orr
Food for Peace

1880–

At the close of the eighteenth century, the English economist Thomas Malthus argued that, while the world's population increased by geometric ratio, its food supplies would only increase arithmetically. What then was only a theory has today become a grim reality. The human race stands on the brink of a catastrophe that will engulf all nations regardless of how rich or powerful they are. The question facing thoughtful men today is can something be done on a worldwide scale to prevent hunger? That the answer is a cautious yes is the work of many men; but the most important is Baron Boyd-Orr.

John Boyd-Orr was born on September 23, 1880, into the family of a lower middle-class building contractor in Kilmaurs, Ayreshire, Scotland.

He was a brilliant student, both at preparatory school and at the University of Glasgow, even though his family was poor and he had to be self-supporting. After beginning as a theology student, he shifted fields and became a medical doctor, then decided upon a life dedicated to research, and took a doctorate in science.

As a graduate student, Boyd-Orr became fascinated with new problems developing in the field of metabolism and nutrition, particularly animal nutrition. He threw himself into basic research and, by 1914, had achieved a nation-wide reputation of such stature that he was named director of the new Institute of Animal Nutrition at Aberdeen. Then the war came.

Believing that Germany was responsible for starting the war, he raised, commanded and took with him into the battlefields of France a unit of the Officers Training Corps. He served with conspicuous bravery, winning both the Military Cross and the Distinguished Service Order, and he won them both without killing anyone; he was a doctor, dedicated to the saving of lives.

When the First World War was over, Dr. Orr returned to the Institute of Animal Nutrition. During the war years, work at the instutute had come to a standstill; it lacked adequate financial backing. Few men like to knock on doors and ask for money. None care to spend endless hours haunting government offices in search of aid. Yet for twenty years Boyd-Orr did these things and his own research as well. He made his institute famous for its work, and he himself became a Fellow of the Royal Society; he raised more than a hundred thousand pounds in the form of endowments and, in so doing, learned the art of diplomacy, which was to prove useful later.

During the years in which he was studying the effects of various diets upon the health of animals, Boyd-Orr was also doing research on problems of human nutrition. In 1925, he demonstrated that supposedly healthy children showed a remarkable improvement in both health and physique when given a pint of milk at school each day. Ten years later, in a pioneer study entitled *Food, Health and Income*, he conclusively showed that more than one-third of the population of Great Britain was living on a deficient diet, and that the major reason for malnutrition was poverty. As a result of his research, Boyd-Orr became one of the world's foremost authorities on nutrition and he was also one of the most active. He founded and edited a journal, *Nutrition Abstracts and Reviews*, wrote three books and a vast number of articles. He served on six important commissions and committees, ranging from the National Advisory Committee on Nutrition to a League of Nations committee to investigate world nutrition. At the same time, he carried on his own research. In 1935, he was knighted for his services to British agriculture.

When war came to England in 1939, Boyd-Orr, as a member of the War Cabinet Committee on Food Policy and as a professor of agriculture at Aberdeen University, was responsible for making decisions about the kind and amount of food necessary to keep armies in the field.

In April, 1945, the United Nations was established and, under its auspices, several agencies were set up to grapple with some of man's fundamental problems. When the Food and Agricultural Organization was founded, at its first conference, Boyd-Orr was unanimously elected director-general.

As head of the FAO, Boyd-Orr worked as tirelessly as ever. The task to provide food for the world was a crucial effort, if there was to be peace. His job was to lead, to present constructive proposals, to offer stimulating criticism and to be on hand when needed. Time and again he proposed ways and means to contend with problems, only to see his proposals voted down by the nations involved. Most disappointing was the rejection of his plan for a World Food Council with executive powers; that is, a body that would take over food surpluses and try to cope with want on a global scale. But he knew some triumphs, too.

In his years with the FAO, Dr. Orr ruined his health by overworking. In 1948, he retired from the FAO but not from an active life. He wrote a book that year, *Food—the Foundation of*

World Unity, and he was elected president of The World Movement for World Federal Government.

In 1949, Boyd-Orr was the unanimous choice of the Nobel Committee to receive the Prize for Peace for his leadership of the FAO and for his efforts on behalf of world federalism. If food and peace can be equated, it followed that Boyd-Orr had made a real contribution toward peace.

In the years following the bestowal of the Prize, awards of all kinds were showered upon him. He was raised to the peerage, becoming Baron Boyd-Orr of Brechin (his motto, "Let there be bread"). In 1961, at the age of eighty-one, he was made president of the World Academy of Science and Art in Jerusalem.

At the time of writing, Baron Boyd-Orr is alive and, as might be expected from so indomitable a figure, still involved in searching for the ephermeral but vital goal: peace.

Ralph J. Bunche
Mediator Extraordinary

1904–

RALPH J. BUNCHE was born in a room above his father's barber-shop, in Detroit's Negro ghetto, on August 7, 1904.

It was impossible for Ralph's father to adequately support his family; few ghetto fathers could afford a ten-cent haircut. As a result, time and again, the family verged on starvation.

When Ralph was ten, the family moved to Toledo, Ohio, where his father hoped to find factory work. But he was ill with tuberculosis and his wife suffered from rheumatic fever. Eventually, enough money was scraped together to consult a doctor, who advised the family to leave Toledo with its rigorous winters and settle in the Southwest.

For the poverty-stricken Bunche family, the Southwest was almost as remote as the moon. But the family possessed one priceless resource, Grandma. Earlier she had decided Ralph would be educated, and he had not missed a day of school since; with the parents sick, she had to find the strength to carry the burden of the family. She met the challenge head on. Penny by penny the fare was accumulated, and in late 1914, the family moved again, a long and weary trip that was in vain. Ralph's mother died in the fall of 1915 and his father three months later.

Grandma then decided to move to Los Angeles, and in early 1916 the family began moving westward. On the way they stopped at one town then another to enable Grandma to earn the money to keep them going.

Settled in Los Angeles, Grandma saw to it that Ralph went to school. He wanted to work, but there was little argument. If a Negro boy was to have a chance, he must be educated.

In his four years at Jefferson High, Ralph made the debating team, the baseball, football and basketball teams, and he was graduated with honors—one of the top ten boys in his class.

He was offered an athletic scholarship to the University of California at Los Angeles and considered refusing it. He was eighteen years old—healthy and strong—and it was time he took the burden of responsibility from Grandma's shoulders. But her will was unshakable.

In 1927 he was graduated *summa cum laude* from UCLA and with a tuition scholarship to Harvard University. But could he in good conscience go East and leave his family to fend for itself? Grandma had done enough. So, in the little apartment in the Negro section of town, there were arguments, Ralph's arguments. Grandma didn't bother to argue much; for her the question was settled. Secure in her certainty that her grandson would go on after so many years of struggle, she went to sleep one night, not long after his graduation from college and never woke up.

Ralph went east, and the years at Harvard were good for him. For the first time he felt free to discuss the problems of the Negro in America with the knowledge that his audience would be understanding and sympathetic.

Upon graduation with his M.A. degree in 1928, he decided to teach. He received a number of job offers, many from all-white schools, but he knew his training could best be put to use in a Negro school, and he accepted a position at Howard University in Washington, D.C.

Bunche was a good teacher, and his classes were filled to overflowing. By 1938 he had worked his way up to full professor. Earlier, he had been offered a fellowship to travel in Europe, Asia and Africa. He accepted it as an opportunity to collect material for his doctoral dissertation. When he returned, he wrote the dissertation and in 1934 became the first Negro in American history to be awarded a Ph.D. in political science.

By 1941, when war came, Bunche's reputation had grown to such an extent that he was named senior social scientist in charge of research on Africa in the Office of Strategic Services.

His work in the OSS brought him to the attention of highly placed government officials. In 1943, he was made chief of the African section of the State Department and, in 1944, was appointed territorial specialist in the Division of Territorial Studies.

When the war finally drew to a close, Bunche was appointed one of the American delegates to work on the United Nations Charter. What later became the official United States plan for trusteeships was largely a product of his efforts.

By the spring of 1948, war had broken out in the Holy Land between the Arabs and the Jews over Israeli statehood—a war that could engulf the whole Middle East and bring in the major powers.

The dispute was submitted to the United Nations, and the Swedish diplomat, Count Folke Bernadotte, was appointed as its official mediator. Bunche was asked to serve as Secretary of the United Nations Special Committee on Palestine.

In the midst of efforts to end the war, tragedy struck the negotiating committee. Bernadotte was assassinated by a group of fanatics in Palestine.

With the death of Bernadotte, Bunche became the acting mediator and personal representative of Trygve Lie, Secretary-General of the United Nations. The entire responsibility for working out a truce now rested upon his shoulders.

What Bunche had to do was to extract as many concessions as possible from the victorious Israelis—yet granting their basic demands—and find some way to save face for the Arabs. At first, he simply got the Arabs and Israelis to talk while he listened. Then, slowly, he began to intervene.

He got the Arabs to believe that he regarded their bargaining position as equal to Israel's. Finally he managed to persuade them that, like it or not, Israel existed as a state and they might as well accept that fact. From the Israelis he managed to extract a number of small concessions.

The negotiations at last bore fruit, and in January, 1949, the war between the Arabs and Israelis was ended. When the conferences were over, the Israeli representative said to Bunche, "I cannot become the spokesman for the world, but you have earned the thanks of the world for your superhuman labors." And the Arab spokesman added, "Mr. Bunche, you are one of the world's greatest men."

Ralph Bunche returned home a national hero. There was a ticker-tape parade in New York, an endless round of receptions and an invitation to meet President Harry Truman at the White House. Out of this meeting came the offer of a position as Assistant Secretary of State, the first time such a high post was offered to a Negro. But Bunche refused. His refusal constituted a sad reflection upon race relations in the nation's capital. He had, he said, "served my exile there," (in Washington) and added, "now I prefer to live as a free man."

For his unstinting efforts to achieve peace, Bunche was awarded the 1950 Nobel Prize. He was the first black man to be so honored.

Now in his sixties, he continues to work for the United Nations, where he occupies the second highest position, and for world peace. He speaks of returning to teach one day, for he believes teaching as important as diplomacy.

From the slums of Detroit to world prominence: For a white man, taking advantage of all the opportunities offered, it would be a triumphant career; for a Negro, with few opportunities to take advantage of, it has been an incredible one.

Léon Jouhaux
Peace Through International Labor

1879–1954

Born in Paris in 1879, the son of a common laborer in a match factory, Léon Jouhaux's early life was one of economic privation. In the last quarter of the nineteenth century, the fate of the working man was a cruel one. There was no protection against industrial accidents, no insurance if accidents occurred, no unemployment relief and no organized group to represent the workers in their relations with the management. The employers paid the workers as little as possible, and often the worker's paycheck was too small to support his family.

When Léon was twelve he had to give up school and go to work. Work was hard to find, but after a long search he found a job in a paper mill. There followed a round of jobs. Finally, when he was sixteen, he joined his father, brother and sister in a match factory. In that same year, 1895, a group of working men met at Limoges and established the Confédération Générale de Travail (General Confederation of Labor), the labor organization destined to become the most powerful in France.

Work in the match factory was hard and dangerous; not even the most elementary precautions were observed to protect the workers' health. Moreover, since the state owned and controlled the business, the workers were forced to accept whatever limitations the state imposed upon their political activities and even upon their personal lives. This, Jouhaux found out when he helped organize a demonstration intended to attract public attention to the plight of the workers. He was fired for engaging in "political" activities. The confederation (CGT) took up his case and got him reinstated. As a result, he joined the union.

He then settled into a dual role of laborer and trade unionist. Bound to his workbench during the day, he attended union meetings in the evenings, worked for the union during periods when he was laid off from the factory, accustomed himself to speaking in public and private gatherings and slowly began to gain public recognition.

In 1906, Jouhaux was elected a delegate to the National Confederal Committee, the governing body of the CGT, and his union activities increased. Several years later, he was elected treasurer of the CGT; and in 1909 when the secretary-general was forced to quit, Jouhaux, then twenty-nine, was elected to fill his position.

At this time, the CGT was rich only in promise, and powerful only in potential. But forces were at work that would shortly catapult the union and Jouhaux into positions of power and prestige. For one thing, in France in the years after the turn of the century, the economy was thriving and even the poor laboring men were making some gains, despite the most determined opposition. Then when war came in 1914 and there were far more jobs than men to fill them, labor was in a good position to negotiate.

Obviously, a negotiator was needed. That was the function of the CGT carried out by Jouhaux. So during the war years and after, workers joined the CGT in increasing numbers until by the mid-twenties there were over two-and-a-half million members.

Before the war, Jouhaux was an ardent advocate of revolutionary policies. But when the full impact of war burst upon France, and its existence as a state appeared seriously threatened, Jouhaux was forced to consider his position. The result was a shift from revolutionary to evolutionary Socialism. Jouhaux became a member of the Labor Committee of the Ministry of Munitions and several other government bodies.

When Germany surrendered in 1918, Jouhaux was appointed to represent France as a labor delegate at the Versailles Conference. There he was largely responsible for formulating Part XIII, the so-called International Labor Charter, of the peace treaty.

However, when the treaty emerged from the hands of the diplomats, it appeared to him highly discriminatory against labor; he resigned his post, quite disenchanted. However, Jouhaux never opposed the concept of an organization dedicated to world peace, and he served as a French delegate to the League of Nations from 1925 to 1928.

Meanwhile the success of the Russian Revolution in 1917 acted as a tremendous stimulus to the advocates of international Communism, particularly within the ranks of organized labor in Europe. In France, the working class had always been the most radical element in the social structure, and the Communists found it comparatively easy to infiltrate the CGT. With the ending of the war, Jouhaux was challenged by the Communists for leadership of the union which he had helped to make the most powerful force in French labor.

His response to the challenge was to expel the entire Communist membership of the CGT. Since French labor was quite radical and the decision to expel the Communists was largely Jouhaux's own, it is surprising he managed to remain in power. But gradually the workers who left the CGT out of sympathy for the Communists came back and Jouhaux's prestige was enhanced.

Jouhaux was still secretary-general of the CGT when France fell to the Nazis in 1940. Rather than flee to safety in England, he went to the south of France, where he engaged in the resistance movement and managed to escape capture for eighteen months. During that time, he organized resistance units among the trade unionists, established a courier system with Britain, and helped set up counterespionage posts in German headquarters areas. But he was finally captured and deported to Germany.

After the war, Jouhaux returned to France to resume his place as head of the CGT. However, during the war, while Jouhaux's attention was centered elsewhere, the Communists had moved into positions of power within the union. Intent upon using it to further their own ends, they had reduced Jouhaux to little more than a figurehead. They then set out to deliberately wreck the Marshall Plan under the guise of a strike for higher wages. Aligning himself on the side of the Government in opposition to the strike, Jouhaux helped to break it, but in 1947 he left the union he felt he could no longer control.

Following World War II Jouhaux played an outstanding role in the work of international cooperation. In 1946 he was a member of the French delegation to the United Nations, but the International Labor Organization, the only League of Nations organization to survive World War II, claimed his fullest attention. He saw in the work of the ILO the possibility of lowering the tension which leads to war by a process of social leveling on an international scale.

Jouhaux was awarded the Nobel Peace Prize in 1951. Because the Storting never states why the Prize is awarded, one can only conjecture. He may have received the award for a number of reasons: saving the French labor movement from Communist domination; supporting international disarmament in the 1920's; his work with the ILO during the 1930's and after World War II; and his activities in the United Nations.

Three years after receiving the Peace Prize, a heart ailment proved fatal. He died in Paris in 1954.

Albert Schweitzer
The Great Humanitarian

1875–1965

ALBERT SCHWEITZER was born on January 14, 1875, in Kayserberg, a little town in the province of Alsace. His father and mother were French. A few years before, at the conclusion of the Franco-Prussian War, that province had come under German rule, and so, technically, Schweitzer was German by birth.

Albert showed few signs of precocity in his youth, except for music. He began to play the piano at the age of five and at eight he learned to play the organ. When he was nine, he could play it well enough to substitute for the organist in the village church! At that age his father sent him to a secondary school in nearby Münster for a year, then to the gymnasium at Mülhausen, where he concentrated on history and science, then his favorite subjects.

If Schweitzer had devoted all his time to his studies while attending secondary school, he might have been a top student; but he did not. He was also being trained in music by Eugène Münch. Münch was a great teacher and awakened Schweitzer's early interest in Bach, an interest which led to some of Schweitzer's most important publications. His instruction was so thorough that after graduating from the gymnasium in 1893, Schweitzer made a trip to Paris where he played for Charles Marie Widor, one of the greatest organists of the day, and was accepted as his pupil.

That same year, Schweitzer enrolled at the University of Strassburg. There he immersed himself in philosophy and theology, either subject generally considered sufficiently difficult to fully engross the average student's time. In addition, each day he practiced for hours on the organ.

In May of 1898, he passed his theological examination. Schweitzer did brilliantly and was given a scholarship to study for the degree of Licentiate in theology.

However, Schweitzer decided first to obtain the degree of Ph.D., and in October of 1898, he went to Paris to study philosophy, to write his doctoral dissertation and to study the organ.

In the Münster Valley where Albert was born, the physical stamina of the Schweitzers was legendary. Albert was able to work all day and all night without intermission, except to eat, and often contented himself with a single meal. He seemed a stranger to fatigue. Had he not been so strong, despite his extraordinary brilliance, he could not have achieved what he did. When one considers that, by the time he was twenty, Schweitzer was fluent in Greek, Latin, Hebrew, German and French; that he was recognized as one of the most brilliant students at the University of Strassburg; that he wrote his doctoral dissertation based on one of the most difficult of all philosophers to understand; that by the time he was twenty-seven he was a professor himself and one of the greatest concert organists in Europe, one gains some understanding of the man's extraordinary qualities.

It took him four months to write his doctoral dissertation and by mid-1899 he passed the oral examinations, received the degree, and set about putting his thesis in order for publication. The thesis was, by all accounts, excellent. It was published under the title, *The Religious Philosophy of Kant.*

He was then free to pass his second theological examination and become curate at the Church of St. Nicholas in Strassburg, to begin writing another thesis for the Licentiate in theology and to pursue his studies of the origin and meaning of the Gospels. In 1900, he took his degree of Licentiate with a thesis on the "Problem of the Last Supper"; he published a book, *The Mystery of the Kingdom of God,* in 1901; wrote another thesis that same year on Christ's messianic ideas, and in 1902, accepted an appointment as professor in the Department of Theology at the University of Strassburg.

In 1904, Schweitzer made a decision that altered the entire course of his life, eventually carrying him from a fame justly won to the seeming obscurity of French Equatorial Africa. He decided to become a doctor and to practice medicine in Africa. His mind made up, Schweitzer walked across the campus from the Department of Theology to the Department of Medicine at Strassburg and enrolled as a medical student.

Schweitzer's accomplishments in the next seven years, unless well-documented, would scarcely be credible. Besides his medical studies, he continued to lecture in divinity; preached every Sunday at St. Stephen's; undertook the organ part of the Paris Bach Society's concerts each winter and those of the Orféo Català in Spain; and gave concerts throughout France and Germany. In 1906, he published two books, *The Gospel of the True Organ* and *The Quest of the Historical Jesus,* probably his most important in Biblical criticism. While a medical student, he also completed his first history of the Pauline doctrine, *Paul and His Interpreters,* revised and enlarged *The Quest of the Historical Jesus,* and, with Charles Widor, prepared an edition of Bach's preludes and fugues for the organ. To top the impossible, he took a "first" on his medical examination, paid for by performing on the organ at the French Musical Festival at Munich! After that, all that was needed was to write a thesis for the doctorate, spend a year as an intern, collect money to finance the dispensary he intended to establish, and he was ready to leave for Africa.

For a proud man, the most difficult aspect of all this was collecting money. He suffered a number of humiliations in his efforts but he remarked "the kindness I experienced . . . outweighed a hundredfold the humiliations which I put up with." The important thing was, he got the money necessary to finance his voyage to Africa and to establish a hospital and keep it running for a year.

In 1912, he married Helene Bresslau, who studied nursing to help her husband. In March, 1913, Schweitzer and his bride set out for Lambaréné, a missionary station on the Ogowé River, in Gabon, French Equatorial Africa. The choice of site for the location of the hospital had been made on the strength of a map and the advice of an Alsatian missionary in Africa. For a distance of from one to two hundred miles upstream and downstream patients could be brought to the hospital by canoe. The natives, suffering from such diseases as malaria, sleeping sickness, leprosy, cardiac complaints, hernia and dysentery, would use the facilities if they could get there; hence, Lambaréné was ideal.

Schweitzer had thought, before leaving Europe, that buildings would be available at Lambaréné for a hospital; but they were not, so he began his African career beneath the burning sun. From the first, patients flocked to him for help. Carried up the bank from the river by relatives, or hobbling on improvised crutches, they sat or lay on the hard-packed dirt as the doctor moved among them, cleansing and bandaging festering wounds, or rebandaging old ones, sometimes marking a patient for an operation.

The heat of the tropics is enervating, and even a man of Schweitzer's enormous energy tired quickly. He was compelled to seek shelter in a broken-down chicken coop. The room was thoroughly scrubbed, the walls whitewashed, the floor disinfected. In such humble surroundings, but protected from the sun, Schweitzer established the first room of a hospital that within a few years became world-famous.

Schweitzer's hospital wasn't run like other hospitals. With an instinctive understanding of the psychology of the natives, he attempted, as much as possible, to make their stay in the hospital like being at home.

People normally recover much more swiftly in familiar surroundings. Thus the beds of the wards were wide enough to accommodate not only the patient, but the relatives or friends who brought him. Men and women were allowed to sleep in the same ward, and to do the cooking for themselves and the patient on the hospital grounds.

It sounds unsanitary; to a degree it was. But the virtue of allowing such wide latitude led to Schweitzer's success. Normally, native Africans avoided white doctors and their sterile hospitals. Schweitzer's hospital they understood, and as the fame of *Oganga* (medicine man) spread over the province of Gabon, the stream of patients became a torrent; by the time Schweitzer retired, over a million and a half had received treatment!

With the advent of war in August, 1914, it mattered little that the work in which Schweitzer was engaged benefited humanity; he was an enemy alien, an Alsatian. The French military commander in Gabon placed the doctor and his wife under house arrest for several months and closed down the hospital. However, Schweitzer simply couldn't remain quiescent and watch people die nor, as it turned out, could the French Commandant. The doctor and his nurse-wife were soon adjudged to be "nonpolitical" and they were allowed limited freedom to go on with their work.

Even such limited freedom could not last indefinitely. In 1917 Schweitzer and his wife were sent back to Europe. After being interned in several different camps in France, the Schweitzers were exchanged for French prisoners of war in the spring of 1918.

The next two years marked the nadir of Schweitzer's career. He managed to support himself, his wife and his daughter, by practicing as a physician in the municipal hospital in Strassburg. But he was physically exhausted, ill and dispirited. Everything he had done at Lambaréné had apparently been destroyed. Moreover, he was horrified at the barbarity of the war that had achieved nothing.

At this critical juncture in his fortunes, Schweitzer received an unexpected invitation from the Archbishop of Sweden, Nathan Söderblom, to deliver a series of lectures at the University of Upsala, in the spring of 1920.

He arrived in Sweden a tired and depressed man. But, thanks to the care and hospitality of the Söderbloms, he quickly recovered his health and spirits and, as a result of the help of the Archbishop, Schweitzer was engaged to give further lectures and some concerts. With the money he earned, he was able to pay off his most pressing debts and saw his way clear to return to Lambaréné.

He had been gone seven years. As the launch carrying Schweitzer and his party glided around the last bend of the river and approached the landing, everything appeared well. The white buildings still stood on the three small hills, the doctor's house seemingly was untouched. But it was an illusion. The jungle had reclaimed its own. Everywhere there were vines and snakes and dry rot. Undaunted, Schweitzer began again, and soon the gleaming white buildings were restored.

The rebuilt hospital was drastically overcrowded. Schweitzer hoped that the overcrowding of the hospital was merely temporary, but the legend of the "big doctor," who could "kill" people, repair what was wrong and bring them back to life, had spread for hundreds of miles across Equatorial Africa. Schweitzer finally realized that the hospital would be permanently crowded. So he decided in 1926 to move the hospital two miles up the river where land was available for indefinite expansion. After some three years of incredible labor, the transferral of patients to the new hospital finally began.

During the 1930's the fame Albert Schweitzer had turned his back on many years before again caught up with him, this time enormously enhanced. Then he had been the brilliant young scholar and organist. At this point, he also became known as a great humanitarian, a selfless man who had dedicated his life to helping others. As such, he caught the imagination of the world. Tributes poured in; and he received far more invitations to lecture and to give concerts than he could possibly accept.

During World War II, the doctor managed to keep his hospital open. He returned to Europe late in 1948, so famous that it became a burden. Everywhere he went, in Europe or on his one trip to the United States, he was followed by hordes of reporters and cameramen. He was constantly solicited for interviews and deluged with invitations to address various groups. In 1951, he received the peace award of the West German Association of Book Publishers for his efforts to build an "ethical world society." That same year he received the distinguished honor of being elected to the French Academy. He was back in Lambaréné in 1953 when news came that he had been awarded the delayed Nobel Peace Prize for 1952.

He was too busy at the hospital to make the trip to accept the Prize but he sent a letter to the Nobel Committee expressing his appreciation and saying that he intended to use the Prize money to establish a leper colony adjacent to the hospital. His letter was published in the papers and, when it became known what he intended doing with the $33,840 Peace Prize, an even larger sum was raised by popular subscription. It was given to the doctor when, in 1954, he went to Oslo to deliver the traditional Nobel lecture.

His reception at Oslo can only be described as magnificent. Students put on a torchlight procession and crowds lined the streets to see the man many considered "the greatest figure of our time." The King and Queen invited him to the palace, and leading dignitaries vied for the honor of having him as their guest.

In his Nobel lecture, Schweitzer pleaded for mankind to rise above the thoughts, the passions that lead to war and to acquire the will to peace. He pointed out that through his command of physical forces, man has become superman, but, he added, "we are becoming inhuman in proportion as we become supermen." At the close of the lecture, he quoted the words of the Apostle Paul, "If it be possible so far as depends on you, live in peace with every man," and he added, "these words are not only for individuals but also for nations."

Returning to Lambaréné, he began work on the leper colony which, before his death, contained some three hundred persons. He continued, as he had for the past forty years, to minister to the sick, he practiced continuously on his beloved organ-piano, and he wrote constantly, publishing three books in 1960-61, one, *Peace or Atomic War*, dealing directly with the most crucial problem of our era.

He died in Lambaréné on September 4, 1965.

George C. Marshall
Reconstruction of Europe

1880–1959

In the ugly little village of Uniontown nestled beside the Monongehala River in Pennsylvania where he was born on December 31, 1880, George C. Marshall spent his boyhood years and dreamed of the day when he would be a general in the United States Army. Such dreams are often forgotten, but Marshall's was not; and at seventeen, the tall, handsome boy with clear blue eyes and sensitive mouth, pug nose and freckles, entered the Virginia Military Institute.

He had never done well in school; his teachers had found no trace of the computerlike mind for which the future general would one day be noted. There was some doubt that he would graduate from VMI, but he did. He was even elected Senior Class Officer and First Captain of the Cadet Corps.

Marshall immediately applied for a commission in the regular Army, and in 1901, he became a second lieutenant. A year later he was sent to the Philippines for his first tour of duty in a foreign country, and then, after two fairly exciting years, he was ordered to Fort Reno in the Oklahoma Territory.

There he came to the attention of Captain Malin Craig, who was later to become chief of staff. Craig recognized Marshall's potential as a leader and saw to it that he was sent to the School of the Line at Fort Leavenworth, Kansas.

The boy, who had been thought almost dull back in Uniontown and an average cadet at VMI, emerged from the School of the Line with a brilliant record.

In 1913, Marshall was again sent to the Philippines. And again he was lucky. General J. Franklin Bell made Marshall his aide-de-camp and saw to it that he was promoted to captain.

During World War I, Marshall's reputation grew. He helped plan the strategy that led to victory in the battles of St. Mihiel and the Argonne Forest. And when the Germans finally surrendered, he was credited with being "one of the five or six men most responsible for the success of the American arms in France. . . ." But when the war ended and the Army shrank to its peacetime strength, Marshall, temporarily a brigadier general, wound up a major and faced again the slow arduous process of working his way up through the ranks.

Then after tours of duty as aide-de-camp to General John J. Pershing and in China on September 1, 1939, Marshall achieved the highest position a general in the American Army can aspire to. He became chief of staff.

That day Germany invaded Poland, and immediately England and France declared war on Germany.

In the War Department, his face gray with strain, Marshall worked incredible hours. Decisions had to be made instantly, many of them involving the survival of the country. Congress had passed the first peacetime draft in American history and thousands of men were pouring into the services, but they had to be trained and equipped and bases established.

The attack on Pearl Harbor came on December 7, 1941. When it was over, it had united the country as nothing else could have.

With the exception of Franklin Delano Roosevelt, no man in the United States was more responsible for American victories in the years between 1941 and 1945 than Marshall. No major strategic decision was made without his advice; the details, once the decision was made, were left up to him and the other senior officers involved.

When the war ended, Marshall asked to be retired. He was sixty-five years old, his job was done and he was tired. Like most great generals he had come to hate war with a bitter passion, and he wanted to forget.

In October, 1945, he was retired. Two months later he was called upon by President Harry S Truman to become ambassador to China. He was asked to find a formula that would resolve the conflict between the Chinese Nationalists of Chiang Kai-shek and Mao Tze-tung's Communists: a formidable task.

Initially, it looked as though he might succeed. Nineteen days after he arrived, the Government and the Communists signed a truce. Six weeks later, a formal agreement was drawn up to reduce the size of the opposing armies and to merge them together. Unfortunately, neither Chiang nor Mao wanted peace. The truce, the agreement, were simply façades behind which their forces maneuvered for position.

Had Marshall stayed in China, his great personal fame might have prevented a renewal of the war. But he decided to fly to the United States and deliver a personal report to the President. When he returned a few weeks later, he was confronted with a rapidly deteriorating situation. A little more than a year after he was assigned to China, Marshall returned to the United States, his mission a failure. However, on February 21, 1947, he was appointed Secretary of State.

It cannot be said that Marshall was a great Secretary of State; he was a great general, and the roles often conflicted. Trained in a milieu where a commanding officer's wish was tantamount to a command, Marshall's mind did not adjust to the world of politics. He was used to ordering people, not asking them, and a secretary cannot give orders either to Congress or to foreign diplomats.

But if he was not a great Secretary of State, he was a good one and at Harvard University in June, 1947, he proposed a plan (first developed by President Truman) that changed the course of postwar history.

In 1947, Europe was on the verge of economic catastrophe. Large portions of her industrial plants had been ruined, her currency was unstable. In many areas people were unable to feed and clothe themselves. This situation invited political anarchy and was, in fact, proving fertile ground for the development of Communism.

The European Recovery Program, or the Marshall Plan as it came to be called, was simply an invitation to Western Europe and Russia to state their needs. The United States, motivated in part by fear of a Communist take-over in Europe, was prepared to foot the bill. As Marshall pointed out, "Our policy is directed not against any country or doctrine, but against hunger, poverty, desperation and chaos."

Russia and its satellites refused, but sixteen nations responded to the invitation. Within three months of the time Marshall delivered his address, they had reached an agreement. The bill came to $6.8 billion.

In January, 1949, worn out from the endless round of conferences he had to attend, Marshall resigned as Secretary of State. But in 1950, unable to refuse the call of duty, he accepted the position of Secretary of Defense.

He was the logical man for this position. War had erupted in Korea, and the Army had to be rebuilt. Marshall accomplished the job, but he was getting old and tired. He was seventy and ready to end forever his active participation in public affairs. In September, 1951, assured that a good man would take his place in the

Department of Defense, he retired. Eight years later, on October 16, 1959, at the age of seventy-eight, he died.

In the course of his event-filled life, Marshall had been accorded many honors. The last and, for a man grown sick of war, the greatest, was the Nobel Prize for Peace which was awarded to him in 1953. That a noted warrior should win a peace prize appeared paradoxical. But before there could be peace, men like Hitler had to be destroyed, and Marshall helped do that. Furthermore, it was the Marshall Plan that saved the peace in Western Europe after 1947.

Lester Bowles Pearson
The United Nations as a Peace-Keeping Force

1897–

LESTER BOWLES PEARSON was born on April 23, 1897, at Newtonbrook, Ontario. His father, a Methodist minister, and his mother were descended from Irish immigrants.

Lester did so well in school that, at sixteen, he was able to enter the Methodist Victoria College of the University of Toronto. He might have finished, but in 1914 war broke out in Europe, and Canada was immediately involved. In the middle of his second year, he left school and enlisted in the Medical Corps.

If he hoped to emerge from the war a hero, reality shattered his dreams; he never saw combat. After initial training, he was sent to Greece. The British and French were bogged down at Salonika; there was little or no fighting, and Pearson experienced that other side of war: boredom. Fortunately, his father had a friend who was a general. Strings were pulled, and Lester was transferred to England and given a lieutenant's commission in the Royal Flying Corps.

Here, at last, he stood on the threshold of glory. Nicknamed "Mike," because as his senior officer put it, Lester wasn't a very belligerent name for a fighter pilot, he crashed on his first solo flight. Uninjured by the crash, a few days later the would-be eagle was hit by a bus and had to be invalided home.

Back home, Lester found a position in Chicago and embarked upon a business career. However, rapidly coming to the conclusion that he wasn't executive material, and even if he was, his lack of education would stand in the way, he applied for and was granted a scholarship at Oxford University.

He began his studies in history in the fall of 1920, and his years at Oxford, Pearson later maintained, were the happiest of his career. Life in the ancient town moved at a quiet, even pace; for the serious student—and Pearson was that—there were lectures to attend, long lists of books to read, requirements of tutors to satisfy, debating clubs and—during leisure hours—long, rambling walks through nearby fields and woods.

Advanced study opened the door to a profession he could enjoy, and one in which he could find satisfaction. At the conclusion of his second year at Oxford, he returned to Canada and was offered a position as lecturer in history at the University of Toronto.

He enjoyed teaching and the students enjoyed him. Possessing an agreeable personality, delighting in argument and devoted to his students, he quickly became one of the more popular professors on campus.

On one of his many trips to Ottawa to collect materials for his Ph.D. dissertation, Pearson met the head of the Department of External Affairs who, impressed by the younger man, attempted to convince Lester to take the examination being held the following year for first secretary in the diplomatic service. Although Pearson was happy with his teaching position, he was curious to see how well he could do.

Pearson thought little of the test he had taken for fun until he was notified he had placed first!

It was difficult to decide if he should give up a secure teaching career for an uncertain future with the diplomatic service. But possibilities of advancement, far in excess of anything in the academic world, were opened up to him. So he elected to gamble and, in August, 1928, made the move to Ottawa.

Settled in the capital, Pearson began a slow, upward climb through the hierarchy of the diplomatic service. He did a variety of routine jobs, served on various economic commissions, wrote reports and moved a long step forward when he was sent to London, in 1935, as deputy to Vincent Massey, Canadian High Commissioner.

However, he still did little but routine jobs. One exception was his work at Geneva. He was called upon to represent his country at various conferences held there, and once, for a brief period, he even acted as Canadian representative to the League of Nations. His role was minor, but it was his one really responsible position before World War II.

When war came, Pearson, still in London with the Office of the Canadian High Commissioner, found his days an endless round of conferences and meetings in which strategy was developed for interlocking Canada's economic and military strength with that of England's. Eventually, however, he was called home to become assistant to the Under Secretary for External Affairs.

He did not remain long in Ottawa. After the entry of the United States into the war, Pearson was assigned to the Washington delegation as the number-two man. Later, he became a minister and when a Canadian embassy was established, Pearson became Canada's first ambassador to the United States.

As victory for the Allies became certain, Pearson began to involve himself more and more in the various plans for the postwar world. He was associated with the talks held at Dumbarton Oaks; at San Francisco he helped draft the Charter of the United Nations. In addition, he was one of the leaders in establishing the United Nations Relief and Rehabilitation Administration and the Food and Agricultural Organization. These activities and others served to distinguish him from rank and file diplomats, and he became an international figure. He was seriously considered for the position of Secretary-General of the United Nations; but, politics, among other things, prevented his election.

Pearson's work in the United Nations during this period is well-known. Less well-known is the fact that he was an architect of the North Atlantic Treaty Organization (NATO).

It was in answer to the overt threat posed by Russia in the post-war years that the Prime Minister, Louis St. Laurent, in a speech largely written by Pearson, made the suggestion that contributed to the development of NATO. St. Laurent pointed out that if the tragedy of Czechoslovakia was not to be repeated, it would be necessary to develop a regional alliance as a counterweight to aggressive Communism.

The new organization, as visualized by Pearson and embodied in St. Laurent's speech, was not to be specifically military, but was to serve as a focal point for greater economic cooperation, for unified political action and as a means of bringing moral pressure on Russia to preserve peace. Unfortunately, the alliance, when it did come into being, tended to emphasize the military. As a result, although acceptable under the terms of the United Nations Charter, and necessary in terms of the cold war, NATO tended to vitiate the meaning of the world organization.

Even so, Pearson always believed that "the most important thing I participated in was the formation of NATO." Had the United Nations been given the military power to enforce its decisions, as at an earlier time Pearson had argued it should, then NATO would have been unnecessary.

Between 1947 and 1956, the United Nations dealt with a number of issues that could have led to war. Three of these, the partition of Palestine, the Korean War and the Suez crisis, were perhaps the most important, and with all three the name of Lester Pearson is intimately connected.

As Under Secretary and later Minister for External Affairs, Pearson ranked as Canada's permanent representative to the United Nations, and automatically took command whenever he attended its deliberations.

The nature of the Palestine crisis can be stated simply. After World War I, Great Britain accepted a mandate over Palestine which was populated by both Jews and Arabs who were bitter enemies. During the 1920's and 1930's, but especially during World War II, millions of Jews, who regarded Palestine as their homeland, flooded into the area. Great Britain attempted, and failed, to keep peace between the Arabs and Jews. Then, in 1947, tired of the problems involved, and incapable of handling them, Great Britain notified the United Nations that she intended to relinquish the mandate.

The Palestine crisis might have led to World War III had not a special United Nations Commission, including Canada, recommended partition of the Holy Land.

When it became obvious that the United Nations Assembly was going to accept the resolution for partition, Pearson argued that mere acceptance wasn't enough; careful study was needed to see how the method for partitioning would be applied. As a result of his argument, the assembly set up a four-nation working group, with Pearson representing Canada, and this group devised the plan that led to the creation of the State of Israel.

As had been the case with Palestine, Canada had no vital interests involved when the Communists invaded South Korea in June, 1950. But when the Security Council adopted a resolution calling for a cease-fire, and called upon participating members for troops to repel the invasion, Canada was quick to respond. The General Assembly was anxious to bring the fighting to a close as quickly as possible, so a committee of three, including Pearson, was drafted to serve on a cease-fire committee. Two years later, when the truce ending the war was finally signed, it closely followed the outline of the committee's report.

The crisis over the Suez Canal in 1956 seemed as dangerous to world peace as the Korean War. Involving most of the major powers, it temporarily split the Western alliance of England, France and the United States. Canada was forced into the ticklish position of making a choice between her allies across the Atlantic and her powerful neighbor to the south. That Canada successfully walked the tightrope and the United Nations managed to weather the crisis was largely due to the work of Lester Pearson.

When Israel, France and England attacked Egypt for seizing the Suez Canal, the United States immediately introduced a resolution in the Security Council calling for a cease-fire and a withdrawal of the invading forces. France and England vetoed the resolution and the United States opted to carry the fight before the General Assembly where the resolution carried 65 to 5, with Canada abstaining.

In a speech delivered immediately afterward, Pearson pointed out that since the resolution was, in his opinion, fair, Canada could not vote against it, yet it was inadequate, so she could not vote for it. What would happen if France and England refused to comply with the terms of the withdrawal resolution? Force would mean world war. And even if they did withdraw, what then? In six months the same situation might recur. What was needed, he urged, was a United Nations force to maintain peace while the political problem concerning the canal was settled.

The United States promptly adopted Pearson's suggestion. However, someone was needed to press the idea and Pearson was the logical choice. He had been president of the assembly, he was an old hand in the United Nations, and he was on a first-name basis with half the delegates.

Convinced that the assembly would go along with his suggestion, he introduced the Canadian resolution; that the Secretary-General, within forty-eight hours, present to the assembly "a plan for the setting up, with the consent of the nations concerned, of an emergency international United Nations force to secure and supervise the cessation of hostilities."

The Canadian resolution passed 57 to 0. Fortunately, France, England and Egypt were all looking for ways out; the creation of a police force gave them an opportunity to retire gracefully. War was averted. The gratitude of the world was indicated by the choice of Lester Pearson for the Nobel Peace Prize in 1957.

After the defeat of his Liberal party in 1957, Pearson used his energy and talents toward a revitalization of the party. When Louis St. Laurent retired that same year, the party selected Pearson to take his place. This meant that if the Liberals could win the next general election, Pearson would be the new Prime Minister.

The assault began immediately and it was successful. On April 22, 1963, Lester Pearson went to pay the traditional call upon the Governor-General to be sworn in as Her Majesty's first minister in Canada, a position he held until his retirement in the spring of 1968.

Reverend Dominique Georges Pire
A New Life for Refugees

1910–1969

If only the rules are considered, it is impossible for a Nobel winner to nominate himself. Even so, if an individual believes he warrants the Prize and if he has a qualified friend or acquaintance who can nominate him, he can rate as a candidate. Normally, of course, such a candidate has little chance of winning. But one of the most innocent of men, desperately in need of money, manipulated and won his nomination, and a village whose only hope was Father Dominique Pire benefited from his act of courage.

Georges Charles Clement Chislain Eugène François Pire was born on February 10, 1910, in Dinant, Belgium, the eldest of seven children. As a child, he was obstinate, a practical joker, a collector of stamps and cigar bands, and not distinguishable from his playmates.

It is sometimes a mixed blessing for a boy to have a schoolteacher for a father. In Georges's case, he was taught by his father both in and out of school, and while he learned methodical habits of study, he found his father stern and demanding. However, the boy did quite well, even winning a number of prizes for scholarship.

The family, refugees at the beginning of World War I, returned to Belgium in 1918. In 1926, Georges decided to become a priest.

That decision shocked his parents. Georges was a good boy, even a religious boy, but he had never given the slightest hint of intending to enter the priesthood.

Compared to the outside world, life in a monastery is hard. Georges became Brother Henri Dominique. His room was a small, whitewashed cell containing a washbasin, an iron stand, a narrow wooden bed and a straw mattress. His clothes—the white, flowing habit of the Dominicans; his job—to study, to learn, to pray and to wait on tables.

For Brother Henri Dominique, however, the compensations of the monastic life far outweighed the disadvantages. He was surrounded by a group of men dedicated to the service of God. There was security, a sense of belonging, of being caught up in something greater than an individual. Finally, there was no coercion. The novices were free to leave the monastery whenever they pleased. It was a full year before Brother Dominique took his first vows, and they were only for three years. At the end of that time, he could still leave.

Apparently, there was never a question in Brother Dominique's mind. In 1932, he took his final vows. That year, Brother Dominique was sent to Rome to study at the Dominican University, the Angelicum, for a doctorate in theology.

In Rome, Brother Dominique became Father Pire, held his first Mass and then was ordered to La Sarte, a monastery at Huy,

Belgium. At the monastery, Father Pire worked hard on his dissertation, and, at twenty-six, he was awarded his doctorate in theology.

Much to his surprise, he was assigned to teach the Dominican Brothers at La Sarte. A modest person, he did not yet feel qualified to teach. He applied for and received permission to spend another year of study and then, more confident, returned to La Sarte where he settled as a teacher. He was a good one, but he was not happy. More interested in practical matters than teaching, it seemed to him he was marking time while events passed him by.

In the summer of 1940, German armies smashed into Belgium, and the roads leading south into France were choked with refugees. Like the others, Father Pire fled. But France, too, was overrun and was no longer a refuge, so Father Pire returned to La Sarte.

At the monastery, the quiet Dominican priest went on with his lectures as the havoc of war raged across Europe. Seemingly withdrawn, occupied with his lectures and with scouring the countryside for food for the children of the villages, as well as with ministering to the spiritual wants of the people, who could suspect that the man of God had become a courier for the famed *maquis,* the French guerillas fighting the Germans? Yet the white-robed figure, moving through the shadows of night, ostensibly on errands of mercy, again and again carried in his pockets messages that would have condemned him to instant death had he been caught. When the war was over, he was rewarded with medals and ribbons: Medaille de la Reconnaissance Nationale, Medaille de la Résistance and Croix de Guerre.

In 1946, Father Pire was relieved of his teaching duties and appointed curé of La Sarte—a disappointing assignment. Repeatedly he had asked that he be allowed to work with those uprooted by war. But in the Dominican Order, one vows obedience, and so he took up his duties. Father Pire devoted himself to the people of his parish and in meeting their needs, he moved down from the plane of abstract intellectual pursuits to the muddy affairs of men where, in fact, his heart really lay.

However, for the restless spirit of Father Pire, success as a curé was not enough compared to the needs of hundreds of thousands of displaced people engulfed in pain and hopelessness.

He heard an address by a man who had resigned his position working in the refugee camps for the International Relief Organization, because of a feeling of futility. He suspected that the nations contributing money to the IRO were only interested in worthwhile refugees; that is, the healthy ones. If a refugee had a trade or profession, and if he was free of disease, he might be an asset to a country and would be welcome. But if he were old, unhealthy or missing a limb, then it seemed that, as far as the nations of the world were concerned, he could rot in one of the camps.

The speech was a call to action for Father Pire. In 1949, the Aid for Displaced Persons was organized in Huy, and Father Pire left for Austria to view firsthand the conditions of the people who were to form his larger parish.

There, he was introduced to the tragedy of the homeless and the hopeless; to the terrible pain of the loneliness of the aged for whom no one cares; and to young people, injured by war. He shuttled from camp to camp on an endless treadmill of world indifference. He was also introduced to nobility, as men and women of the IRO struggled with rules and regulations to deal with the flood of people pouring into the camps.

Father Pire found that the IRO was doing a magnificent job. In ten years it moved over five hundred thousand refugees out of the camps, but one hundred and sixty thousand were found superfluous by the nations of the world. For these, the old and the lame, there were strict, precise rules. They needed help, and there was no help. So, they were shelved by the IRO under the terrible rubric of "Nothing to be done."

The IRO officials had their orders guiding admittance of immigrants to various nations and they had to obey. There would be little mercy in sending an immigrant to a country where he would find the doors closed against him.

Returning to La Sarte, Father Pire plunged into his double

role as parish priest and head of Aid for Displaced Persons. He began soliciting help through every possible medium and, with heartbreaking slowness, the response came. By the end of 1949, he had a thousand sponsors and had to expand his headquarters to accomodate gifts of clothing, food and medicines.

Shortly after organizing Aid for Displaced Persons, Father Pire came to the conclusion that in spite of everything he was doing to feed and clothe the victims of war, it was not enough. Homes were needed, particularly for the elderly.

In September, 1950, a converted bakeshop in Huy became the first home for aged DPs in Europe. A number of others were to follow, and then, in 1956, he inaugurated a new scheme, the European Village.

The European Village was an extension of what he was trying to do for the aged, to get people out of the refugee camps and, by integrating them into a community, give them a sense of dignity and security.

But there were serious problems before he could establish the first village at Aachen, Germany. He had to get the permission of the German Government, and then assure the inhabitants of Aachen that in no way would the village constitute a threat to them. It took weeks of hard work before he succeeded. Once the village was established and the villagers began to be integrated into the larger community, prejudice tended to disappear, as Father Pire had suspected it would.

Inspired by what he had accomplished at Aachen, Father Pire turned his attention to establishing other villages. By 1958, five villages had come into existence. His attempt to establish a sixth village led to the Nobel Prize.

In 1944, the little Jewish girl, Anne Frank, had been murdered by the Nazis in the Belsen concentration camp. She was fourteen when she died and, in 1958, fourteen years later, Father Pire wanted to establish a village in her memory. The problem was money. Every cent coming into Aid for Displaced Persons was desperately needed elsewhere. The Ford and Rockefeller Foundations had denied his requests, and the Nobel Foundation had informed him it did not give money, except for the Prizes. Obviously, there was only one answer; he must be awarded the prize!

He found a gentleman qualified to recommend him and, as supporting evidence that he was worthy, he sent the Nobel Committee a leaflet he had had printed for public consumption, describing the work that Aid for Displaced Persons was doing.

In 1958, he was invited to dinner at the Norwegian Embassy and engaged in conversation by an elderly gentleman from the Nobel Foundation. He was invited to Oslo to give an account of what he was doing. It all appeared very promising, and then he read that no award would be given in 1958. Disappointed and a little disgusted, he gave up.

Then the reporters called with the news that he had won, and he brushed it aside as a joke, since the official telegram wasn't delivered until later, due to some mix-up. The reporters called again; his secretary at the headquarters telephoned and the news was confirmed. Father Pire had joined the immortals.

The award was given to him on December 10. He was gratified that by its bestowal his work had received world recognition. Even more gratifying was the check, approximately forty-five thousand dollars! Now, indeed, there would be an Anne Frank Village.

Since the awarding of the Prize to Father Pire, the question has often been asked, should he have won it? Was his work truly for international peace? But it must have appeared to the Nobel Committee that if there is going to be international peace, men must learn, in a broad sense, to love one another. In this regard, no greater man has emerged in the twentieth century than Father Pire.

He died on January 30, 1969, in the Roman Catholic Hospital in Louvain, Belgium.

Philip J. Noel-Baker
A Lifetime Search for Peace

1889–

Like a number of other Prize winners, Philip Noel-Baker had a fortunate childhood. Born on November 1, 1889, in London, he passed his formative years in one of the most secure eras in history (for an Englishman) and in one of the most secure spots on the globe, the British Isles. From childhood associated with politics, Philip was never to be too far removed from the center of power.

He went first to Bootham School, and from there to Haverford College in the United States. Then, having achieved a brilliant scholastic record, he was sent to King's College, in Cambridge.

In 1912, he was president of the Cambridge Union Society and a member of the British Olympic track team. In 1914, having done outstanding work in history and economics, he was well on his way to a distinguished career when World War I began.

A member of the Society of Friends from childhood, Philip had been nurtured on a philosophy of nonviolence. Yet, as a patriotic Englishman, genuinely convinced that Germany was responsible for the war, he could not stand by idly. So in the fall of 1914, he organized and commanded an ambulance unit composed of young men who, like himself, were of the Quaker faith.

Driving an ambulance was difficult and dangerous work. Many drivers were killed and some, like Philip, exhibited conspicuous heroism. He was awarded several decorations, including the Italian Silver Medal for Valor and the Croce di Guerra.

With the end of the war Philip took lodgings in Cambridge and began the arduous study for his final examinations in economics. He was awarded a first class, an honor which opened a number of roads into the future. But what did he want to do?

Across the Channel, in Paris, an attempt was being made to establish a League of Nations, dedicated to preventing future wars. The British delegation included Viscount Cecil of Chelwood, and Viscount Cecil was delighted to have Noel-Baker as his principal assistant. So, in 1919, Philip joined hundreds of other bright young men who had gathered in Paris to assist the leading statesmen of the West in establishing peace.

Philip's work at Paris and later in Geneva, while sometimes arduous, rarely failed to be interesting. Ranging from questions concerning disarmaments—his special interest—to those dealing with refugees, it had the kind of variety that would appeal to an agile and dedicated mind. He was an invaluable assistant to Cecil and later to the first Secretary-General of the League because he spoke, and eloquently pleaded for peace in several languages. Also, his wide experience in Paris enabled him to play an important role in the administration of the League in Geneva. Intimately acquainted with League machinery and the refugee problem, Noel-Baker persuaded Fridtjof Nansen of Norway to set up a bureau of refugees and organized the prestige and power of the League behind Nansen's efforts

In 1924, Noel-Baker accepted a position as the first Cassel Professor of International Relations at London University, and be tween 1924 and 1929 he was enormously productive, writing five books and a large number of essays, articles and reveiws. Then, having been elected to Parliament, he immediately became Parliamentary Private Secretary to Arthur Henderson, Secretary of State for Foreign Affairs, and for the next twenty-five years the name of Noel-Baker was to figure prominently in English politics.

Throughout the 1930's Noel-Baker worked for peace. In 1933, he acted as assistant to Arthur Henderson, who became president of the Disarmament Conference. He was a delegate to the League of Nations; he published extensively in the cause of peace; he lectured for peace and he knew the tragedy of defeat when war came again to England.

During World War II, Noel-Baker served in a variety of capacities. He was a member of the Foreign Office Advisory Council on Aliens and was Joint Parliamentary Secretary to the Minister of War Transport. Then, when the Labor Government took office at the close of the war in 1945, he moved up to become Minister of State in the Foreign Office and a British delegate to help draft the United Nations Charter at San Francisco; a year later he was a delegate to the First United Nations General Assembly.

Between 1945 and 1959, Noel-Baker held offices ranging from Secretary of State for Commonwealth Relations to commandant of the British Olympic Team, as a result of his participation in Olympic games in the 1920's. He figured prominently in the debates over Suez that took place in 1956, and two years later he published an influential volume entitled *The Arms Race: A Programme for World Disarmament.*

But in Baker's own words, "the greatest honor a man can receive in this world" is the Nobel Prize for Peace and in December of 1959, he received the coveted telegram informing him he had won. It was the capstone of his career; given not for any single effort but for a life's devotion to international peace. At the time of the award he observed to reporters, "If this award to me can help in the smallest degree to bring success for this greatest of all causes, I shall feel that the efforts I have made will not have been in vain," and he went on to comment that the Prize money would be used toward furthering world disarmament.

Albert J. Luthuli
The Struggle Against Apartheid

1898–1967

In December of 1960, the world was informed that Chief Albert John Luthuli of South Africa had been awarded the Nobel Prize for Peace. But who was Albert John Luthuli and what had he done to merit the Prize? Because of lack of accurate information, all the lines of Luthuli's portrait could not be clearly drawn at first, but the picture that finally emerged was that of a great person who well deserved the Prize.

The odds against the baby born at the Seventh-Day Adventist Mission near Bulawayo in Southern Rhodesia in 1898* becoming

*Lutuli did not know the year of his birth. He said it was before 1900; the date 1898 is usually given in accounts of his life and career.

a Nobel Prize winner were so astronomical as to defy calculation. He was the son of a proud people, the descendant of Zulu chieftains and warriors. But pride of birth is no substitute for status rendered inferior by force of circumstance, and in Luthuli's early years, the native African was definitely considered inferior by the white man. If his skin was black, that could be considered conclusive proof that he never would achieve anything: white men would see to that. However, in Luthuli's case they made a profound mistake—they allowed him to have an education.

The Luthulis were not native Rhodesians, but had originally come from Natal, a province of present-day South Africa. In 1908 or 1909 Albert, his mother and his elder brother, Alfred, returned to South Africa. His father had died when Albert was six months old.

In northern Natal, the family settled on a farm owned by a white adherent of the Adventists. Alfred began his duties as an interpreter, and Albert was put to work tending the mission mules.

Had it not been for his mother, tending mules could well have been the end of the road for young Albert. But his mother was determined that he should get an education. There were no educational facilities at the mission; they were available, however, in the ancestral home of Groutville, and so Albert was sent to live with his Uncle Martin—the village chief—to begin his education.

Life in the village of Groutville was exciting for the youth who had known only the discipline of mission life. There were youngsters his own age with whom he could play, there was school, in which he did very well, and finally, as the nephew of the chief and a member of his household, Albert had an opportunity to observe the workings of tribal justice, and to prepare himself, unconsciously, for the role he himself would fill one day.

In 1915, after a year in boarding school, Luthuli entered a Methodist institution at Edendale, near Pietermaritzburg. The teachers, mostly white European, were excellent and dedicated and they inspired in the young man a high regard for the teaching profession, one of the few that were open to black South Africans.

Upon graduation from Edendale, he found a position as principal in a place called Blaauwbosch in the Natal uplands. It sounds like quite a job for a first-year teacher, but as Luthuli remarked wryly, "It was not very impressive—I was also the entire staff." At Blaauwbosch, Luthuli came under the influence of a conscientious African minister who "converted" him from a nominal to a true Christian, and he met and impressed Natal's Chief Inspector for Native Education. At the end of his second year at Blaauwbosch, Luthuli received a scholarship to Adams College.

He spent fifteen years at Adams College, the first two as a student in the teacher-training division, the last thirteen as one of the two African teachers on the staff. He conducted successful courses in Zulu and music, acted as the college choirmaster, taught a course in school organization and, when he left Adams, was acting as supervisor of teachers in training at outlying schools.

Life at Adams was, for Luthuli, a good life. He loved teaching, the opportunity to be of service. He read widely in sociology, religion and political philosophy, and began to involve himself in the affairs of the teaching profession. By 1928, he had become the secretary of the African Teachers' Association and the founder of the Zulu Language and Cultural Society. But, although happy and involved, he was nevertheless an African on a predominantly white staff and he was made to feel the difference; he could not socialize on an equal footing. Second-class citizenship apparently did not inflict much psychological pain upon Luthuli. He was too great a person to be affected, and he possessed, as one writer put it, "the humility of a man who cannot be humiliated. . . ." He could be of service as a teacher, and that was enough, or it might have been had not fate intervened.

For various reasons, domestic affairs were not going well in Groutville, and the village elders, wishing to get rid of their chief, approached Luthuli with the request that he allow his name to be put up for election. Albert refused. For two years, he put off the elders with one excuse or another. Finally, in 1936, the call of his people was so insistent that it could not be ignored or evaded. He capitulated and was elected chief.

As chief of the Umvoti Mission Reserve (Groutville was the administrative center) which covered nearly ten thousand acres and had a population of about five thousand, Luthuli was in charge of all the affairs of the community; these ranged from presiding over criminal proceedings in the local court to trying to reconcile married couples who had been fighting. Once in a while exciting, but mostly dull, Luthuli's work did serve the purpose of opening his eyes to the poverty-stricken lives of black South Africans. As a teacher, he had to a degree been sheltered from economic reality; as a chief, he was not.

Actually, his people were better off than most Africans; their land was better. Still, they lived barely above subsistence level, not because they lacked ambition or intelligence, but for reasons beyond their control. They couldn't, for instance, even farm efficiently because they lacked finances to buy fertilizer and equipment and, since they were black, no bank would lend them money. Government agricultural experts were supposed to advise them as to the best crops to plant, harvesting methods and so forth, but they evaded their responsibilities. Intent upon keeping the blacks in a subordinate position, the whites took every available advantage of their control of the economy.

As a minor chief in a remote village, there was little Luthuli could do to change the economy of South Africa. But, characteristically, neither could he stand by and do nothing, particularly when, by limiting production, the Government moved to peg the price of sugar, the only marketable crop produced in Groutville. It wasn't that Luthuli opposed limited production, it was that the quota system introduced was inequitable. The answer, Luthuli believed, was organization. Under his direction, the moribund Groutville Cane Growers' Association was revived and, using it as a lever, Luthuli managed not only to persuade the Government to change its quota methods; he also persuaded the millers to advance enough money on future crops to ease the burden of planting for the farmers.

Luthuli's success interested other African farmers and, sometime in the late 1930's, he was instrumental in putting together the

Natal and Zululand Bantu Cane Growers' Association. Acting as a counterpart to associations founded by white farmers, it never achieved equal status, but it did wrest a number of concessions from the Government that helped to improve conditions for black farmers.

The founding of the organization also served to make Luthuli's name known to both blacks and whites. In the years between 1936 and 1945, Luthuli became one of the best-known of all black South Africans. This was due to his efforts in the founding of the Cane Growers' Association, as well as his work in preserving the Mission Reserves from whites intent upon taking over the land, and for his involvement in such political organizations as the African National Congress.

The African National Congress was founded in 1912. At first, a mild response to racial inequality, the congress, by a sheer force of circumstances, was forced into a militant position. Luthuli, while an ardent Christian and a believer in nonviolence, had also come to believe that if the Africans were not willing to struggle for their rights they would lose them by default. In 1945, he became an active participant in the Natal section of the congress and was immediately appointed to the executive committee.

In 1949, in response to discriminatory practices that eventually forced all blacks to carry passes even to move from one village to another, the African National Congress adopted a plan aimed at more direct action to secure African rights. They advocated demonstrations, strike action and civil disobedience. Such actions had little or no effect, except to call forth more repressive measures. These elicited countermeasures; the African National Congress organized a one day stay-at-home for all black Africans. The Africans stayed home as planned, but the action achieved little and the congress decided upon a campaign of civil defiance.

Luthuli felt that the congress was not yet well-enough organized to make a success of the campaign. However, the consensus was that the campaign should go forward and Luthuli was forced to agree. The campaign began very well. Huge demonstrations were held, carefully trained volunteers were sent into the cities to disobey discriminatory laws, blacks "forgot" to show up for work, or they "forgot" their passes. The Government struck back. The leaders of the movement, among them Luthuli, were arrested.

Perfectly aware that the strength of a totalitarian Government relies upon its command of force, Luthuli had expected to be arrested. Booked by the police in Durban, after helping them disperse a large and angry crowd that might have caused a riot, he was warned and then allowed to go free. He could not, however, avoid some kind of penalty. Called in by his immediate supervisor, a white man, Luthuli was grilled about his activities in the ANC and informed that such activities were inconsistent with his duties as chief. Luthuli argued that they were not; but he was given a choice: retire from politics or be fired as chief. It was impossible for Luthuli to equivocate, so he ceased being chief in Groutville.

Unfortunately for the defiance movement, rioting did occur in several South African cities. By identifying defiance with riots, the Government was in a position to break the power of the movement. And it did, with deliberate cruelty. Black Africans were murdered and all the power of a modern-day police state was mustered against anyone who dared to defy the Government.

The purpose of the defiance movement was not to foster riots; it was inalterably opposed to them; it did not want bloodshed. The point was not to kill Europeans, or destroy their property, but, if possible, force the whites to recognize that the blacks, too, had rights. So when rioting began, the movement took steps to bring its campaign to a close. Luthuli, whose integrity as an opponent of white power could not be challenged and whose prestige as an organizer and leader was perhaps greater than any other black African, was chosen to do the job. In December of 1952, he was elected president-general of the African National Congress and brought the defiance campaign to a close.

For the next several years, Luthuli was in the forefront of the fight for equality between the races. The totalitarian Government often used its power against him. Late in 1953, he was subjected to a ban; that is, he was debarred from entry into all the larger centers of South Africa and was not allowed to attend public meetings. In 1954, he was subjected to another ban, one confining him to the Groutville area, and, in December, 1956, he was arrested in Groutville. The charge? High treason! The crime? Eventually, he was accused of 104 crimes.

Although charged with treason, Luthuli was not brought to trial immediately. He did go to jail, but was soon discharged and back exercising his leadership of the ANC. Formal leadership did not last long; in 1959 he was again banned, again limited to Groutville—this time for five years.

1960 was a terrible year for black South Africans. Throughout the nation, there was police suppression of the most elementary rights of the blacks. A wave of riots and violence took place in the major cities, and was repressed with extreme brutality; at Sharpeville scores died when police fired into a crowd. Confined to Groutville, Luthuli called for a day of mourning to commemorate Sharpeville, then led a campaign to burn pass books, the hated symbol of black South African inferiority.

The Government responded with another wave of arrests, and again Luthuli was thrown into jail; this time to stand trial for treason. He was convicted on two counts, of burning his pass (which he did), and of disobeying a law by way of protest. The sentence, six months in prison, was suspended because of his health. Exiled back to Groutville, he was there when informed that he had been selected as the 1960 Nobel Laureate for Peace.

The Government considered the selection of Luthuli an insult; as one official spokesman put it: "The government fully realizes the award was not made on merit and must necessarily rob the Nobel Peace Prize of all its high esteem in the judgment of objectively minded people." Perhaps there weren't many "objectively minded" people in the world, because a cry of indignation went up when the Government refused Luthuli a passport. In the face of the outcry, he was finally given a ten-day pass restricted solely to Oslo.

So it was that a black man, dressed in his costume as chief of the Amakholwa tribe of Zulus, stepped before the rostrum in the hall of the University of Oslo to accept his Prize and to deliver what one writer called "the most heart-rending lecture in the annals of the Nobel Prize." The theme of his lecture was simple, its implications as wide as all mankind: How can there be peace, justice and honor in a world that betrays the dignity of man to preserve outworn ideologies? It was a question that still remains to be answered.

Returning to his home in Groutville, Luthuli published a marvelous autobiography *Let My People Go*, in 1962, and in that same year the Government imposed a rule of silence on him, forbidding Luthuli to speak out on any subject. In 1964, the ban was renewed for another five years.

As the years slipped on toward the end of his life, Luthuli's eyesight began to fail, and he became increasingly deaf. On July 21, 1967, he was hit by a train when crossing a bridge closed to pedestrians. Already suffering from ill health, the injuries he sustained were more than he could survive. He was buried on July 30 at Groutville, in the valley of the Umvoti River. Could he have heard the words of the burial service of the Congregational Church, perhaps the single word that would have thrilled him most rang out as he was lowered into his grave: *Uhuru!*(Freedom!)

Dag Hjalmar Agne Carl Hammarskjöld
Peace in the Congo

1905–1961

In San Francisco, in 1945, it was thought that the dawn of a new age began with the founding of the United Nations. Dedicated to the concept of nations guided by world law, a charter of conduct was framed and a Secretary-General elected to lead the way. The Secretary-General, who above all others was best qualified to make reality of the world's dream of peace, died in a plane crash in Northern Rhodesia.

Dag Hjalmar Agne Carl Hammarskjöld was born July 29, 1905, in Stockholm, Sweden. The first Hammarskjöld to win recognition was a cavalry captain who was knighted by Charles IX, in 1610. Thereafter, the destiny of the family was indissolubly linked with service to the crown and, through the crown, to the state.

The family fortune had been lost by unwise speculation, and in his youth, Dag's father, Hjalmar, had turned to the study of law, and to such good effect that, by the turn of the century, he was Minister of Justice. The very picture of a patriarch, stern and commanding, austere and a bit remote, he impressed his sons with his unshakable integrity and utter conviction that duty and service were the natural standards of a Hammarskjöld.

When his father was appointed governor of Upland, the family moved from Stockholm to Upsala. Dag attended the gymnasium and university, and his academic record was one of the best in a hundred years.

After graduation, Dag became one of a group of brilliant young economists, later to earn the name of the "Stockholm School," who were busily engaged in developing the theories that were to spur the development of Sweden as a welfare state. As Secretary of the Royal Commission on Unemployment, Dag was able to help translate some of the suggestions of the group into legislation dealing with the problem of unemployment.

Hammarskjold, shortly thereafter, accepted an appointment as Under Secretary to the Minister of Finance, the top civil service position in the Department of Finance. It was an enormously responsible position. The Minister of Finance must defend the Government's position in Parliament on all financial matters. If he were ill-informed, or inaccurate in his analysis of economic forces at play, the Government would be subject to attack, and could even be overthrown. Hammarskjöld's job was to make sure that this didn't happen.

It was a demanding job, but Hammarskjöld met the demand with apparent ease and with enough time left over to indulge his favorite forms of recreation, literature and music. Intimately acquainted with the literature of France, Germany and England as well as Sweden, he also developed an easy familiarity with their histories, architecture and music. He read constantly for diversion and became, almost as a by-product, a deeply cultured man; one able to transcend any form of nationalism that might have interfered with his work at the UN.

When war came to Europe in the fall of 1939, Sweden immediately proclaimed neutrality as she had in 1914. But this war had a definite impact upon Sweden's economy. Cut off from Europe and with goods of all kinds at a premium, the Government had to pass stringent legislation to avert inflation. One of the jobs devolving upon Hammarskjöld was to write the necessary laws and help to establish a price-control board. Partially due to Hammarskjold's legislation, Sweden managed to keep her economy on an even basis.

Sweden was hardly neutral in her sympathies during the war. Norway had been invaded, her Government was in exile, and at the risk of arousing the wrath of the Germans, Sweden did what she could to lend a helping hand. Credits were arranged to support the exiled Government and negotiations were begun to reestablish Norway's economy as soon as the war was over. For his part in these activities, Hammarskjöld was later awarded the Grand Cross of the Order of St. Olav, Norway's highest award.

When the war ended in 1945, Sweden, like the other nations of Europe, faced the drastic problem of adjusting its economy to meet the changing conditions of the postwar world. It was soon necessary for Sweden to renegotiate her trade agreements with the United States. Chosen to head the delegation sent to Washington, Hammarskjold was such an able negotiator that, when the Marshall Plan was put into effect in 1947, he was appointed Sweden's top representative at Paris where the meetings were held to decide how much the United States would loan each country.

Under the terms of the Marshall Plan, the European nations involved had to pledge maximum self-help and maximum mutual aid. Self-help fell within the province of the internal affairs of the various nations. Mutual aid, however, called for an organization that would act as a governing body in terms of the allocation of funds loaned by the United States, as well as seeing to it that the nations did everything possible to help each other. Thus the Organization for European Economic Cooperation came into being.

As a member of the executive committee, which directed the affairs of the OEEC, Hammarskjöld played a crucial role in Europe's miraculous recovery from the war. As the years passed, his reputation as an impartial, able administrator grew by leaps and bounds. In 1953, when Trygve Lie of Norway was forced by pressure from Russia, England, France and the United States to submit his resignation as Secretary-General of the United Nations, France presented the name of Hammarskjöld with some hope of acceptance.

Hammarskjöld had not expected the nomination, nor did he think there would be any chance of his being elected, if nominated. Then a telegram arrived from the president of the Security Council informing him of the nomination by the council, subject to the approval of the General Assembly.

Hammarskjöld was forced to make a difficult decision. Should he sacrifice a successful career for what might be ignominious failure in the service of mankind? There could only be one answer. He cabled the Security Council a reluctant acceptance.

The post to which Hammarskjöld was elected in the spring of 1953 was an almost impossible one. The United Nations had developed into a forum where the great powers maneuvered constantly to gain an advantage over one another. If the Secretary-General initiated a policy appearing to favor the West, he became to the Russians a lackey of capitalism. If he initiated a policy apparently favoring the Russians, he was thought soft on Communism. If he initiated any policy, as Trygve Lie had, there were those who thought he was attempting to become too powerful; if he did not, he was accused of being wishy-washy. Even if he moved to avert a war he was sure to step on someone's toes.

In the years that followed, the reputation of Dag Hammarskjöld reached giant, and to ardent nationalists, alarming proportions. To many, unfamiliar with the inner workings of the world organization, he *was* the United Nations; the tireless wonder-worker who, time and again, pulled the world back from the brink of catastrophe. In the Middle East, in the Orient—wherever the tensions of the cold war exploded into strife—Hammarskjöld was on hand to argue, to cajole and to suggest rational alternatives. The burden of work he assumed was staggering, the crises he had to face were enough to snap the nerve of an average man, the alternatives to some decisions he was forced to make simply unthinkable. Yet, somehow, he endured, though he was hated by many because he was impartial. By 1961, he was being flayed by the Soviet Union which demanded a troika in place of a single man as Secretary-General; the United States was unhappy with him, as were England and France. He might have overcome all this displeasure, but the crisis in the Congo was to result in his tragic death.

The Belgian Congo had remained immune to the wave of anticolonialism that had swept over Africa after the close of World War II. Other African nations gained their freedom; the Congo appeared content under the rule of Belgium. Then, suddenly, in 1959, riots broke out and the Congolese demanded freedom.

Belgium suggested a plan whereby self-government would be granted; a handful of natives would be integrated into the Government, and then, year by year, a few more would be added until full control passed into native hands. However, the Congolese became impatient with waiting and, finally, Belgium agreed to grant full independence on June 30, 1960.

Unfortunately, while in control of the Congo, Belgium had not trained the Congolese in self-government; there was no established bureaucracy; control of the Army was in the hands of the military chiefs. Within weeks a struggle for power developed.

The first strong man to appear was Patrice Lumumba, the Prime Minister. Lumumba, personally endangered by the excesses committed by the Army, which was running wild, wired Hammarskjöld asking for military assistance.

This was the first time that an appeal had been made directly to the UN for military aid and Hammarskjöld had to make the crucial decision of complying with or refusing the request. If he refused, there could be no doubt that the great powers would intervene. To maintain the neutrality of the Congo in the cold war, to keep her from becoming a pawn of the great powers, Hammarskjöld decided to risk commitment.

Initially, the great powers, including Russia and the United States, agreed to UN intervention. Then, as the weeks passed into months, each of the great powers began to break the consensus as it discovered that what it considered its vital interests were being injured by the UN force. Russia was being blocked from unilaterally aiding the Congolese Government. Belgium was dragging its feet about leaving the province of Katanga, which in turn was attempting to secede from the Congo. The United States, fearing the Russians, was quietly backing the Belgians. Criticism of Hammarskjöld was mounting from every side. Russia was demanding his resignation; Russia and France refused to pay their share of the expenses of keeping a force in the Congo; and the United States, which was footing the bill, demanded that the UN force be used to support Colonel Joseph Mobutu, a new strong man who had overthrown Lumumba and had probably had him murdered.

The attacks upon Hammarskjöld reached a new low in international politics. Premier Nikita Khrushchev appeared on the floor of the Security Council to denounce the Secretary-General and the role of the UN in the Congo. Behind the scenes, the United States was especially bitter because Hammarskjold was urging the UN force to maintain a position of neutrality in Congolese internal politics, hoping that a unified nation would emerge.

That Hammarskjöld's morale slipped under the circumstances was perhaps natural. Then, by a vote of 83 to 11, the General Assembly asserted its confidence in him and his leadership and his spirits rose again. But it is possible that the recovery was more on the surface than deep inside. For one thing, in the summer of 1961, he made out a will. Two days before leaving for the Congo he arranged to dispose of his personal documents if he should die. He took with him on the flight just one book, the *Life of Christ*, in which his oath as Secretary-General was later found. Premonition of death, or coincidence? No one knows.

The occasion for the trip was an invitation from Cyrille Adoula, who had become Prime Minister of the Congo in 1961, for Hammarskjöld to meet with Moise Tshombe, head of the Katanga provincial government, and try to work out an agreement whereby Tshombe could come to terms with the central government. The position of the UN was that there should be one ruling body in the Congo, located at Léopoldville under Adoula; and that Katanga, which provided sixty per cent of the Congo's resources, should not be allowed to secede. Fighting had broken out between the UN troops and the Katangese, and if the fighting were not settled, it was quite likely that the great powers would involve themselves. That could mean the end of the UN.

The meeting between Tshombe and Hammarskjöld was to take place on neutral ground, Ndola in Northern Rhodesia. Landing at Léopoldville, Hammarskjöld was briefed on the political situation, on the fighting that was taking place, and then he boarded a Swedish Transair charter plane for the trip to Ndola. No one knows exactly what happened after that.

The captain was an accomplished pilot with thousands of hours of flight time to his credit; the plane had been checked thoroughly before departure, and a secret flight plan had been filed. However, within ten minutes of the time the plane took off, word of its departure went out over the international news wires.

At 10:10 that night the lights of the plane were sighted over the airport at Ndola; but it never landed, and the people at the airport thought the pilot was either going to wait until daybreak to land or had decided on a new destination. Between twelve-thirty and one-thirty a bright flash was seen in the sky. Unfortunately, no one bothered to investigate and it wasn't until 1:10 Monday afternoon, September 8, that the wreckage was found.

The crash was investigated time and again and three possible answers emerged: mechanical failure, pilot error or sabotage.

Hammarskjöld's body was carried home to Sweden and he was buried beside his father in Upsala.

That fall, the Norwegian Storting posthumously awarded him the 1961 Nobel Prize for Peace, the only posthumous award yet made. Others may have deserved the Nobel Prize after their death, but no one more than Dag Hammarskjöld. He had given his life for peace.

Linus Carl Pauling
The Nuclear Test Ban Treaty

1901–

In 1945, with the exploding of an atomic bomb at Alamogordo, New Mexico, a completely unprepared world found itself thrust into the atomic age. Most of the eminent scientists were aware of the dangers the age posed, and a few attempted to interject a note of rationality into the ghastly arms race that began in the postwar world. Linus Pauling was one of them.

Pauling was born on February 28, 1901, in Portland, Oregon. His father, a pharmacist, was of German descent; his mother, Scotch-English.

As a result of reading, Pauling became interested in science when he was ten or eleven. He first collected insects and minerals and then, at age thirteen, he was introduced to the field he was to help transform.

It happened by accident. A fellow student invited Linus to visit him at his home and there he demonstrated some chemical experiments. Fascinated by what he saw, that same evening, using a chemistry book that had belonged to his father (who had died when Linus was nine) and material gathered from his mother's kitchen, he carried out some experiments of his own. These elementary experiments opened for him an incredibly complex and beautiful world, a world of balance, proportion and symmetry which challenged his understanding and led him on to more than fifty years of exploration and discovery.

As an undergraduate, Pauling entered what is now Oregon State University and studied chemical engineering. Apparently, he found engineering satisfactory; and he displayed such talent that in 1919 the college offered him a one-year appointment as a teacher of quantitative analysis.

However, aware that fascinating new areas of research were being developed in chemistry, Pauling could not rest content with a Bachelor of Science degree in chemical engineering. So he applied for admission to the California Institute of Technology at Pasadena, California.

He spent three years as a graduate student at Cal Tech. In 1925, he was awarded the Ph.D. degree (*summa cum laude*) in chemistry, with minors in physics and mathematics. He had won the highest academic degree and he was still in his early twenties. For the work he wished to pursue he would need the kind of equipment most usually found in universities or colleges, so when he was offered a position as a research associate at Cal Tech, he accepted.

During 1925-26, Pauling became so involved with physical chemistry that he considered specializing in atomic physics. He did not, but as a Guggenheim Fellow in 1926-27, he studied in Europe under the direction of Erwin Schrodinger in Zurich, Arnold Summerfield in Munich and Niels Bohr in Copenhagen. Bohr had already won a Nobel Prize in physics, Schrodinger would win one in 1932. All three of Pauling's teachers were interested in quantum mechanics and guided his investigations in that area. It has been suggested that Pauling's great discoveries stem from the fact that, as a modern theoretical chemist, he took the trouble to learn physics and quantum mechanics which led him to new areas of research.

Returning to Cal Tech, Pauling began the research that was to make him one of the most famous chemists in the world. In 1931 he was the recipient of the first American Chemical Society award of one thousand dollars and "was hailed as a prodigy of American science." By 1936 he had made a number of significant discoveries about the nature of chemical bonds (forces holding molecules together) and had moved on to attack the mystery of proteins. This work, and work done in developing what he called the "resonance theory" (a theory that helped explain the structure of certain molecules) on which he published over a hundred papers and several books, gave him an international reputation. One of his best works, *The Nature of the Chemical Bond*, is considered a classic of modern science.

In December, 1941, war came to the United States and Pauling's life changed profoundly. He had been part of a community of scholars—his hopes, his dreams and his triumphs shared by a multitude of scientists in the nations of the world. But with the outbreak of war, science was no longer international, and scientists ceased being citizens of a common universe. They became, as they have remained, draftees in the service of their respective countries.

So, although he had been a pacifist following World War I, Pauling became a member of the National Defense Research Division. There, between 1941 and 1945, he worked on rocket propellants, on the development of a substitute for human serum in medical treatment, on an oxygen deficiency indicator for submarine and aircraft and on other projects important to the war effort.

He began the work that was to occupy most of his time for the next fifteen years immediately after the explosion of the first atomic bomb. In the fall of 1945, while serving as a member of the Research Board for National Security, he delivered a number of public lectures on the meaning and danger of nuclear war. In 1946, he joined with Albert Einstein and seven other eminent scientists in organizing the Emergency Committee of Atomic Scientists which served as a spearhead in an unsuccessful effort to end nuclear testing. He lectured in foreign countries and he published dozens of articles on world peace and related subjects.

Such activities on the part of even so important a scientist, particularly one who opposed the development of the H-bomb, were certain to be misunderstood, and therefore suspect. In 1950, in spite of the fact that the Soviet Academy of Science rejected some of the most important aspects of Pauling's work, Senator Joseph McCarthy of Wisconsin accused him of being a Communist! The accusation was ridiculous (McCarthy's name became synonymous with wild and reckless charges), but there is no doubt that Pauling's reputation was injured.

In 1952, he was denied a passport by the State Department. This, in spite of the fact that, by then, Pauling was a much sought-after speaker; that he had lectured in great universities ranging from Harvard to Oxford; that he was a member of the executive committee of the Cal Tech board of trustees; that he had been the president of the American Chemical Society; that he had been awarded a number of medals; that he had been commended by his own government for outstanding service during the war.

The scientific world was outraged by this insult to Pauling. But indignation and protests were of scant avail. Pauling was granted a limited passport to travel to specific countries to attend meetings; but he was not allowed unrestricted travel. In 1953, his application for a passport to travel to India was flatly rejected.

However, in 1954, the State Department was faced with a dilemma. In recognition of his outstanding scientific work, that year Pauling was awarded the Nobel Prize in chemistry by the Swedish Academy of Science in Stockholm. Would the State Department dare to turn down his request for a passport to travel to Stockholm? If so, it would place the United States in the same light as Germany, which had denied a passport to von Ossietzky in 1936, and Italy, which had made trouble for Enrico Fermi in 1938. If it did not deny the passport, it would look foolish. Fortunately for America's image in the world, the State Department decided to look foolish. The passport was granted.

In 1957, Pauling made an attempt to place the united opinion of the world's scientists into balance against nuclear testing. On his own initiative, he circulated a petition calling for, among other things, "immediate action to effect an international agreement to stop the testing of all nuclear weapons. . . ." The response from scholars disturbed by the incredible dangers of the arms race between Russia and the United States was immediate and overwhelming. In 1958, Pauling presented to the Secretary-General of the United Nations the same petition signed by 9,235 (eventually more than 11,000) scientists from forty-nine nations. Perhaps persuaded by such a stand among the scientists, the United States, Great Britain and Russia discontinued nuclear testing for a while.

This action on the part of Pauling did not go unchallenged. In 1960, the Senate Internal Security Committee called upon Pauling to explain the purpose and meaning of the petition. Pauling told the committee that the petition was his idea, there was no hidden motive behind it. The committee then asked for the names of the people to whom he had written to help gather signatures and the names of those who responded. Pauling said he was willing to supply a list of people he had written to, but he refused to say who had answered. The committee demanded Pauling change his mind or face a citation for contempt of Congress. Though he could be sent to jail if he was cited, Pauling was adamant in his refusal and, fortunately, the committee decided to drop the matter.

In 1961, afraid she was falling behind the United States in sophisticated weaponry, Russia exploded a few more H-bombs. The United States, in turn, exploded some of its own in 1962 and again the arms race was underway.

Aware that every time a bomb was exploded hundreds of thousands of unborn children received either the death sentence or would be born crippled, Pauling and other scientists were spurred to frenzied activity. Pauling was everywhere—making speeches, debating, writing, arguing, fighting for a cause so great that his own illness (he suffered from nephritis), his tiredness, seemed trivial by comparison. And he succeeded! On October 10, 1963, a partial nuclear test ban went into effect.

It is hardly coincidental that, on the same day, Pauling received a telegram informing him he had been selected the Nobel Laureate in Peace for 1962 (the award was delayed for one year). This is not to suggest that Pauling single-handedly brought the test ban into effect; but, as the great physicist Hans Bethe suggested, "Without his awakening of the public conscience on this issue there would not have been any pressure on governments, and there would not have been any test ban." And Gunnar Jahn, chairman of the Nobel Committee of the Norwegian Storting, in presenting the Prize to Pauling in 1963, stated:

> No one would suggest that the nuclear test ban is the sole work of Linus Pauling. But does anyone believe that the treaty would have been reached if there had been no responsible scientist who, tirelessly, unflinchingly, year in and year out, impressed on the authorities and on the general public the real menace of nuclear tests?

There were those, of course, who regarded the awarding of the Prize to Pauling as an insult to the United States. However, these people conveniently forgot, as the world did not, that the Prize was awarded in the name of a humanity that would suffer somewhat less because Linus Pauling was concerned about its future.

In 1963, after four decades of teaching, Pauling left Cal Tech to join the Center for the Study of Democratic Institutions at Santa Barbara, California. Four years later his restless energies carried him to the University of California at San Diego, and in 1969 to Stanford University. Tall and slender, feeling the weight of years a bit, but as indomitable as ever, one of science's grand old men can look back upon a lifetime of blazing success; of unparalleled achievements.

Reverend Dr. Martin Luther King, Jr.
Integration Through Nonviolence

1929–1968

The grandson of a sharecropper and son of a Baptist minister, Martin Luther King, Jr., was born into relatively comfortable circumstances in Atlanta, Georgia, on January 15, 1929. His father, who became pastor of the Ebenezer Baptist Church shortly after Martin was born, was not wealthy, but his salary was substantial enough to afford his family a decent standard of living. Secure in their home, surrounded by love and affection, his children grew up in a happy, healthy environment.

Martin was lucky in another way. Incidents happened, of course, that served to implant in the boy's mind the concept of "difference"—such as being asked to give up his seat in a bus to a white person, or being rudely told if he wanted service in a shoe store to go to the back; or forced to sit in a certain section of a theater. He was surrounded on every side by tangible symbols of difference, but none ever constituted a challenge to his security as a person.

By the standards prevailing for Negroes in the South in the 1930's and 1940's, he received a good education. Skipping three grades, he was graduated from Booker T. Washington High School at fifteen. There was no question that he would go to college. Morehouse College, located within the city, was the logical choice, and Martin enrolled there in the fall of 1944.

Majoring in sociology and minoring in English, he studied hard, sang in the glee club and chorus, and participated in the work of the YMCA and the National Association for the Advancement of Colored People chapters on campus. He also joined a group of Negro and white students who met periodically to discuss mutual problems, many of them dealing with race relations. This association tended to alleviate Martin's resentment toward the white race; he found that many white students were prepared to be allies in the Negro drive for equality.

Graduating from Morehouse College in 1947, he decided upon the ministry. He was ordained that same year and became assistant pastor of the Ebenezer Baptist Church. Few doubted he would succeed his father. To prepare himself he decided to take advanced work in theology and enrolled at Crozer Theological Seminary—a liberal, interracial institution, in Chester, Pennsylvania.

At Crozer, King was one of the top five men in his class. When he graduated in 1951 with a Bachelor of Divinity degree, he was class valedictorian and was awarded the Pearl Plafkner award for scholarship and the Lewis Crozer Fellowship of $1,200 for two years of advanced study. Martin decided to continue his graduate work, and in late summer, 1951, he entered Boston University as a candidate for the Ph.D.

During the two years he spent in Boston, Martin was offered jobs in various churches and colleges, but the South was home, and southern Negroes were in desperate need of the kind of leadership that could be provided by educated young men. In August, 1954, he left for Montgomery, Alabama, where he became the pastor of the Dexter Avenue Baptist Church.

The first year in Montgomery was pleasant. Martin worked hard establishing himself with his new congregation, completed his dissertation and was granted the Ph.D. in June. Then an event occurred that not only had a decisive impact upon American social history, but served to lift Martin Luther King, Jr., from the obscurity of a small parish in a southern city to worldwide fame.

The beginning was as modest as it was unexpected. On December 1, 1955, Mrs. Rosa Parks, a Negro woman riding on a bus in Montgomery, was asked by the driver to give up her seat and move to the back so that a white person could sit down. It had happened before, many times, but something snapped in Mrs. Parks. She refused and was arrested. The Negroes in the city, the bulk of those who rode busses, were outraged and attempted to negotiate with the bus company to end its policy of racial segregation. Again, as so many times in the past, their attempts were rebuffed. Normally, that would have been the end of the affair; Mrs. Parks would have paid her fine or served her sentence. But this time the Negro citizens of Montgomery organized the Montgomery Improvement Association to spearhead a boycott against the bus company. The philosophy embraced by the association was one of nonviolence. Its most articulate spokesman, the man chosen to be president of the MIA, was Martin Luther King, Jr.

Nonviolence as a philosophy of social change, developed by King to meet the needs of a minority group struggling for equality, draws its inspiration from several sources. Reaching back to Jesus of Nazareth, King accepted the command, "Love thy neighbor as thyself," as an axiom for any group attempting to change social mores without destroying the fabric of society.

From one of the greatest leaders of all time, India's Mahatma

Gandhi, King learned the effectiveness of nonviolent resistance. By preaching love, King made the Negroes' fight a moral issue by placing it squarely within the context of Western morality, which teaches the fatherhood of God and the brotherhood of man. By practicing Christ's command to love and not to hate, the Negroes who followed King put the white man on the defensive. Failure to match the Negroes' humanity convicts the white of hypocrisy. When the white accepts the Negro as a fellow human being, then the fight will have been won.

Finally, one essential aspect of King's theory was drawn from Hegel, a German philosopher of the early nineteenth century, whom King had studied while at college. Briefly, Hegel taught that social movement is generated by the conflict of ideas. A group within society possessing one set of ideas conflicts with a group possessing another and different set of ideas. As a result of the clash a synthesis is formed of both sets, and movement has taken place. The crucial point is that the clashing of ideas is essential. The significance of this theory, applied to the position of the Negro in America, is obvious. If the Negroes quiescently accept what is handed to them, they may remain forever second-class citizens. But if they protest, agitate, make their wants and needs known, they will create the kind of climate that favors change.

During the first few weeks of the Montgomery bus boycott, there was relatively little violence. But, finally, the latent bad tempers of some whites were aroused by the Negroes' persistence; and on the evening of January 30, 1956, the home of Martin Luther King, Jr. was bombed.

Fortunately, no one was injured. Appearing before the excited crowd which swiftly gathered outside, King voiced for the first time his philosophical contribution to the Negro movement. In a ringing voice, a voice that was to become familiar to millions of Americans, he told the crowd he would not encourage them to violence; that those who lived by the sword, died by the sword; that the bus boycott, without violence on the part of the Negroes, would go on.

Strategically, the bombing was a monumental failure. Two

days later the MIA filed suit against the bus company and the city fathers, asking that they be forced to end bus segregation and uphold the rights of Negroes.

On February 21, the city fathers launched their counterattack. One hundred and fifteen leaders of the boycott were indicted and charged with forming a conspiracy to destroy a business, namely, the bus company. The first reaction in the Negro community was one of fear and shock; southern courts have never favored the Negro. Then as the names of the leaders—ministers, teachers, businessmen—became known, fear changed to amusement. Calling the leaders of the community criminals because they were engaged in the boycott was ludicrous. Those indicted went off to jail with smiles on their faces. King, who was delivering a lecture at Fisk University at the time of the mass arrests, hastened back to Montgomery.

The trial moved swiftly to its inevitable conclusion, and the accused were found guilty. But for the city fathers, the victory was meaningless. In an interview, immediately after the verdict was handed down, King was asked what would come next. His answer was simple and to the point. "The protest goes on!"

On June 4, a Federal District Court handed down its decision on the suit brought by the MIA against the city of Montgomery. Bus segregation in Montgomery and in Alabama was declared unconstitutional. The city appealed to the Supreme Court, and on November 14, 1956, the Supreme Court upheld the District Court; the fight was won. On December 20, the mandate reached Montgomery, and the boycott came to an end.

December 21 was an historic day for the Negro in Montgomery. King, and other leaders, rode up front in the buses. The year-long struggle against bus segregation had proven that the use of nonviolent resistance by a determined people was a sharp weapon in effecting social change.

In the months following the boycott, the fame of Martin Luther King, Jr., grew to giant proportions. But, as King pointed out, he did not create the boycott, nor was he alone in leading it to a successful conclusion. Quite the contrary, he became part of the movement after it had begun, he was surrounded by extremely shrewd Negro leaders and backed, always, by the Negro community. King became famous for several reasons. First, his theory of nonviolence added a new dimension to the Negro struggle. It opened a pathway to achieving equality by peaceful means, not only for the Negroes of America, but for minority groups across the world. Secondly, the Negroes were in need of a figure around whom they could rally and they found such a figure in the bright, articulate Dr. King. Third, many whites could identify with Dr. King in their personal fight against discrimination.

The conclusion of the bus boycott was, in a way, the beginning of Dr. King's work. He helped to organize the Southern Christian Leadership Conference, and became its president. He attended the independence ceremonies held in Ghana, Africa. He helped organize the first "March on Washington." He met with President Dwight D. Eisenhower to discuss the problems of the Negroes, took part in voter-registration drives, fought for fair housing and integrated education. He traveled endlessly and made hundreds of speeches. Between speeches, rallies and the care of his parish and family, he found time to write a book about the bus boycott called *Stride Toward Freedom.*

In the course of his brief career, King received a number of awards, ranging from honorary degrees to the Cross of Malta. In 1963, he was voted "Man of the Year" by *Time* magazine. But the greatest honor he received was the Nobel Prize for Peace in 1964.

The nominating committee's reason for submitting his name, even though the Prize is generally given for international peace work, was that the members of the committee felt he was an inspiration to colored people everywhere in their fight for equality and independence. It was suggested that without his moderating influence and dedication to nonviolence, the civil rights issue in the United States could erupt into violence; and *Erbeiderbladt,* the Norwegian government newspaper, concluded that his selection "would give a handshake to all the liberal forces in the American democracy."

Upon receiving notification that he had won the Prize, King refused to accept it as a personal tribute, rather:

> *I do not consider this merely an honor to me personally, but a tribute to the discipline, wise restraint and majestic courage of the millions of gallant Negroes and white persons of good will who have followed a nonviolent course in seeking to establish a reign of justice and a rule of love across this nation of ours.*

The monetary award he received was intended to further the civil rights cause of the Southern Christian Leadership Conference.

Martin Luther King had a dream, a dream where a man's worth depended on the man, not on the color of his skin. It was a noble dream, but King did not live to see its realization. On April 4, 1968, he was murdered, by a white sniper in Memphis, Tennessee.

René Cassin
Defender of Human Rights

1887–

RENÉ CASSIN was lucky enough to survive the terrible shrapnel wounds he received in World War I, and brilliant enough to carve out a career in international law when the war ended. A member of the French Delegation to the League of Nations assemblies and disarmament conferences between 1924 and 1938, he saw his dream of peace smashed by the rise of fascism. In 1940, when France fell, he followed Charles de Gaulle to London and became his assistant.

After the war, he served as head of the Council of State, the administrative high court of France. Then he became a member of the Constitutional Council and, in 1959, a member of the European Court of Human Rights. Since 1965 he has been its president.

A drafter of the Declaration of Human Rights and a leader in its adoption at the United Nations in 1948, he also served as one of the founders of the United Nations Educational, Scientific and Cultural Organization. He was eighty-one when he was awarded the 1968 Peace Prize.

APPENDIX NOBEL PEACE PRIZE LAUREATES

The years in which awards were not given are not listed.

Year	Laureate	
1901	Jean Henri Dunant	Swiss
	Frédéric Passy	French
1902	Élie Ducommun	Swiss
	Charles Albert Gobat	Swiss
1903	Sir William Randal Cremer	English
1904	Institute of International Law	
1905	Baroness Bertha von Suttner	Austrian
1906	Theodore Roosevelt	American
1907	Ernesto Teodoro Moneta	Italian
	Louis Renault	French
1908	Klas Pontus Arnoldson	Swedish
	Frederik Bajer	Danish
1909	Auguste Marie François Beernaert	Belgian
	Baron d'Estournelles de Constant de Rebecque	French
1910	Permanent International Peace Bureau	
1911	Tobias Michael Carel Asser	Dutch
	Alfred Hermann Fried	Austrian
1912	Elihu Root	American
1913	Henri Marie La Fontaine	Belgian
1917	International Committee of the Red Cross	Swiss
1919	Thomas Woodrow Wilson	American
1920	Léon Victor Auguste Bourgeois	French
1921	Karl Hjalmar Branting	Swedish
	Christian Louis Lange	Norwegian
1922	Fridtjof Nansen	Norwegian
1925	Sir Joseph Austen Chamberlain	English
	Charles Gates Dawes	American
1926	Aristide Briand	French
	Gustav Stresemann	German
1927	Ferdinand Buisson	French
	Ludwig Quidde	German
1929	Frank B. Kellogg	American
1930	Nathan Söderblom	Swedish
1931	Jane Addams	American
	Nicholas Murray Butler	American
1933	Sir Ralph Norman Angell Lane	English

Year	Laureate	
1934	Arthur Henderson	English
1935	Carl von Ossietzky	German
1936	Carlos Saavedra Lamas	Argentine
1937	Viscount Cecil of Chelwood	English
1938	International Office for Refugees	
1944	International Committee of the Red Cross	Swiss
1945	Cordell Hull	American
1946	Emily Greene Balch	American
	John R. Mott	American
1947	The American Friends Service Committee	American
	The Friends Service Council	English
1949	Baron John Boyd-Orr of Brechin	English
1950	Ralph J. Bunche	American
1951	Léon Jouhaux	French
1952	Albert Schweitzer	French
1953	George C. Marshall	American
1954	Office of the United Nations High Commission for Refugees	
1957	Lester Bowles Pearson	Canadian
1958	Rev. Dominique Georges Pire	Belgian
1959	Philip J. Noel-Baker	English
1960	Albert John Luthuli	South African
1961	Dag Hjalmar Agne Carl Hammarskjöld	Swedish
1962	Linus Carl Pauling	American
1963	International Committee of the Red Cross	Swiss
	League of the Red Cross Societies	
1964	Rev. Dr. Martin Luther King, Jr.	American
1965	The United Nations International Children's Emergency Fund	
1968	René Cassin	French
1969	The International Labor Organization	

BIBLIOGRAPHY

Angell, Norman. *After All: The Autobiography of Norman Angell.* New York: Farrar, Straus and Young, 1952.

Beal, John Robinson. *Pearson of Canada.* New York: Duell, Sloan and Pearce, 1964.

Bennett, Lerone. *What Manner of Man: A Biography of Martin Luther King, Jr.* Chicago: Johnson Publishing Co., 1968.

Benson, Mary. *Chief Albert Luthuli of South Africa.* London: Oxford University Press, 1963.

Bergengren, Erik. *Alfred Nobel, the Man and His Work,* trans. by Alan Blair. New York: Thomas Nelson & Sons, 1962.

Bretton, Henry L. *Stresemann and the Revision of Versailles: A Fight for Reason.* Stanford: Stanford University Press, 1953.

Butler, Nicholas Murray. *Across the Busy Years: Recollections and Reflections.* . . . New York: Charles Scribner's Sons, 1939.

Callan, Edward. *Albert John Luthuli and the South African Race Conflict.* Kalamazoo: Western Michigan University, Institute of International and Area Studies, 1965.

Chamberlain, Sir Austen. *Down the Years.* London: Cassell and Co., 1937.

Cousins, Norman. *Dr. Schweitzer of Lambaréné.* New York: Harper, 1960.

Evlanoff, Michael. *Nobel: Prize Donor, Inventor of Dynamite, Advocate of Peace.* Philadelphia: The Blakston Co., 1943.

Gumpert, A. G. *Dunant: The Story of the Red Cross.* New York: Oxford University Press, 1938.

Hagedorn, Hermann. *Prophet in the Wilderness; the Story of Albert Schweitzer.* New York: The Macmillan Co., 1947.

Hamilton, Mary Agnes. *Arthur Henderson, a Biography.* London and Toronto: William Heineman Ltd., 1938.

Hammarskjöld, Dag. *Markings.* New York: Alfred A. Knopf, 1964.

Henriksson, Fritz. *The Nobel Prizes and Their Founder.* Stockholm: A. Bonniers, printer, 1938.

Hinton, Harold B. *Cordell Hull, a Biography.* Garden City, N.Y.: Doubleday, Doran & Company, 1942.

Kaplan, Flora. *Nobel Prize Winners.* Chicago: Nobelle Publishing Company, 1941.

Kelen, Emery. *Hammarskjöld*. New York: G. P. Putnam's Sons, 1966.

King, Martin Luther, Jr. *Stride Toward Freedom: The Montgomery Story*. New York: Harper, 1958.

————. *Where Do We Go from Here: Chaos or Community?* New York: Harper & Row, 1967.

Kugelmass, J. Alvin. *Ralph J. Bunche: Fighter for Peace*. New York: Julian Messner, Inc., 1962.

Lash, Joseph. *Dag Hammarskjöld, Custodian of the Brushfire Peace*. Garden City, New York: Doubleday Company, 1961.

Levine, Israel E. *Champion of World Peace: Dag Hammarskjöld*. New York: Julian Messner, Inc., 1962.

Linn, James Weber. *Jane Addams*. New York: D. Appleton-Century Company, 1935.

Lipsky, Mortimer. *Quest for Peace: The Story of the Nobel Award*. New York: A. S. Barnes & Company, 1966.

Lokos, Lionel. *House Divided: The Life and Legacy of Martin Luther King*. New Rochelle: Arlington House, 1968.

Luthuli, Albert John. *Let My People Go*. New York: McGraw-Hill, 1962.

Mitchell, James Leslie. *Earth Conquerors: The Lives and Achievements of the Great Explorers*. New York: Simon & Schuster, 1934.

Noel-Baker, Phillip John. *The Arms Race: A Programme for World Disarmament*. London: Stevens, 1958.

Pauli, Hertha Ernestine. *Alfred Nobel, Dynamite King, Architect of Peace*. New York: L. B. Fischer, 1942.

Pauling, Linus Carl. *No More War!* New York: Dodd, Mead, 1959.

Payne, Pierre Stephen Robert. *The Marshall Story*. New York: Prentice-Hall, 1951.

Pearson, Lester B. *Diplomacy in the Nuclear Age*. Cambridge, Mass.: Harvard University Press, 1959.

Pire, Dominique. *The Story of Father Dominique Pire, Winner of the Nobel Peace Prize*. Translated from the French by John L. Skeffington. New York: E. P. Dutton & Co.

Pogue, Forrest C. *George C. Marshall*. New York: The Viking Press, 1963.

Les Prix Nobel en 1901. Stockholm: Imprimerie Royale, 1904.

Schück, H., and others. *Nobel, the Man and His Prizes*. Amsterdam, New York: Elsevier Publishing Co., 1962.

Söderblom, Nathan. *The Living God; Basal Forms of Personal Religion*. Boston: Beacon Press, 1962.

Stern-Rubarth, Edgar. *Three Men Tried . . . Austen Chamberlain, Stresemann, Briand, and Their Fight for a New Europe; a Personal Memoir*. London: Duckworth, 1939.

Suttner, Baroness Bertha von. *Lay Down Your Arms. . . .* New York: Longmans, Green and Co., 1914.

Valentin, Antonina. *Stresemann*, Translated by Eric Sutton. Foreword by Dr. Alfred Einstein. New York: R.R. Smith, 1931.

241

INDEX

Adam, Madam Juliette, 28
ADDAMS, JANE, 125-129, 133, 161, 162, 238
Adoula, Cyrille, 221-222
African National Congress (ANC), 212, 213, 214
African Teachers' Association, 210
Aid for Displaced Persons, 202, 203, 204
Alsace, 180-181
Alsace-Lorraine, 9
American Chemical Society, 225, 226
American Friends Service Committee, The, 239
ANGELL, NORMAN, 134-138, 238
Anne Frank Village, 203, 204
Arms Race, The, 207
ARNOLDSON, KLAS PONTUS, 45-48, 83, 84, 238
Asquith, Herbert, 141
ASSER, TOBIAS MICHAEL CAREL, 61-63, 65, 238
Association of Scandinavian Free States, 51
Atlantic Charter, 157
Austrian Peace Society, 29, 65

BAJER, FREDERIK, 48, 49-52, 72, 238
BALCH, EMILY GREENE, 159-163, 167, 239
Baldwin, Stanley, 97
BEERNAERT, AUGUSTE MARIE FRANÇOIS, 53-56, 60, 238
Belgian Arbitration and Peace Society, 72
Belgian Congo, 220-222
Bernadotte, Count Folke, 174
Bethe, Hans, 228
Bismarck, Otto von, 9, 46
Boer War, 136
Bohr, Niels, 224
Boulanger, Georges, 80
BOURGEOIS, LÉON VICTOR AUGUSTE, 58, 79-81, 238
BOYD-ORR, BARON JOHN, 168-171, 239

BRANTING, KARL HJALMAR, 82-85, 89, 238
BRIAND, ARISTIDE, 97, 103-106, 110, 132, 141, 238
British Olympic Track Team, 205, 207
BUISSON, FERDINAND, 111-113, 114, 238
BUNCHE, RALPH J., 172-175, 239
BUTLER, NICHOLAS MURRAY, 60, 129, 130-133, 238

Caligula, 115
Canton of Bern, 17
Canton of Geneva, 12
Carnegie, Andrew, 22, 60
Carnegie Endowment for International Peace, 60, 137
CASSIN, RENÉ, 236-237, 239
Castiglione, 2, 3
CECIL, EDGAR ALGERNON ROBERT, 150-153, 206, 239
Chaco War, 148-149
Chamber of Deputies (Belgium), 55
Chamber of Deputies (France), 9, 58, 60, 80, 81, 104-105, 113
CHAMBERLAIN, JOSEPH AUSTEN, 95-98, 102, 110, 238
Chiang Kai-shek, 189
Chiesa Maggiore, 3, 4
Churchill, Winston, 157
Civil War (United States), 130, 167
Confédération Générale de Travail (CGT); *see* General Confederation of Labor
Congress of International Associations, 72
Congressional Government, 75
CREMER, WILLIAM RANDAL, 9, 19-24, 51, 238
Crimean War, 71

Danish Peace Society, 51
Danish War of 1864, 46, 50
Danish Woman's Association, 51
DAWES, CHARLES GATES, 99-102, 238
Dawes Plan, 97, 101, 110
Declaration of Human Rights, 237
de Gaulle, Charles, 236

242

D'ESTOURNELLES DE CONSTANT, BARON PAUL, 56, 57-60, 132, 238
Dewey, George, 34-35
Dewey, John, 162
Dreyfus case, 112-113, 136
DUCOMMUN, ÉLIE, 11-14, 18, 52, 238
DUNANT, JEAN HENRY, 1-6, 7, 238

Edward VII, 24
Einstein, Albert, 226
Emergency Committee of Atomic Scientists, 226
European Court of Human Rights, 237
European Recovery Program, 190
European Village, 203

Famine relief (in Russia), 94
Fermi, Enrico, 227
First Woman's Congress, 161
Food and Agricultural Organization, 170, 171, 195
Food—the Foundation of World Unity, 170-171
Francis Ferdinand, Archduke, 76
Franco-Prussian War, 8-9, 21, 28, 46, 112, 180
French Equatorial Africa, 182, 183, 185
French Society of Friends of Peace, 9
FRIED, ALFRED HERMANN, 63, 64-66, 238
Friedens-Warte, Die, 65
FRIENDS SERVICE COUNCIL, 239

Gandhi, Mahatma, 232
Garibaldi, Giuseppe, 39, 112
General Confederation of Labor (CGT), 177, 178, 179
General railroad strike, 104-105
Geneva Convention (1864), 5, 44, 89
Geneva Protocol (1924), 97
German Peace Society, 30, 65, 115, 144
GOBAT, CHARLES ALBERT, 11, 15-18, 88, 238

"Good Neighbor Policy," 148, 156, 157
Grand Council of Bern, 16
Great Illusion, The, 137
Greenland, 91-92
Grévy, Jules, 79
Groutville, 209, 210, 211, 213, 214, 215
Groutville Cane Growers' Association, 211

Hague Peace Conference (1899), 44, 58, 63, 80, 81, 132
Hague Peace Conference (1907), 63, 81, 87
HAMMARSKJÖLD, DAG HJALMAR AGNE CARL, 216-222, 239
Hegel, Georg Wilhelm Friedrich, 232
HENDERSON, ARTHUR, 139-142, 207, 239
Hitler, Adolph, 116, 143, 145, 146, 147, 162
House of Commons (G. B.), 22, 96
House of Documentation, 73
House of Representatives (U. S.), 155
HULL, CORDELL, 148, 154-158, 239
Hull House, 125, 127, 128, 129, 160

Il Secolo, 39-40
Institute of Animal Nutrition, 169
INSTITUTE OF INTERNATIONAL LAW, 43, 62, 238
International Arbitration League, 21, 22, 23, 24
INTERNATIONAL COMMITTEE OF THE RED CROSS, 238, 239
International Conciliation (organization), 59, 132
International Conciliation (periodical), 59, 132
International Disarmament Conference, 141-142, 207
International Institute of Bibliography, 72
International Labor Charter, 178
INTERNATIONAL LABOR ORGANIZATION, 179, 239
INTERNATIONAL OFFICE FOR REFUGEES, 239

243

INTERNATIONAL PEACE BUREAU, 11, 13, 18, 51, 72, 115, 238
International Red Cross, 94
International Relief Organization (IRO), 202
Inter-Parliamentary Bureau, 17, 18, 88, 89
Inter-Parliamentary Council, 55-56, 60
Inter-Parliamentary Union, 9, 17, 18, 22, 23, 29, 51, 55, 56, 60, 73, 86, 88, 89, 115
Ironworkers Society, 140
Israel, 174-175, 196, 197

JOUHAUX, LÉON, 176-179, 239
Jura-Simplon Railroad, 12, 13

Katanga, 221-222
Kellogg, Asa, 117-118
KELLOGG, FRANK B., 106, 117-120, 238
Kellogg-Briand Pact, 106, 120, 132, 133, 148
KING, MARTIN LUTHER, JR., 229-235, 239
Korean War, 190, 196, 197
Kreiser, Walter, 144-145

LA FONTAINE, HENRI MARIE, 71-73, 238
Lambaréné, 183, 184, 185, 186
Lane, Ralph Norman Angell; see ANGELL, NORMAN
LANGE, CHRISTIAN LOUIS, 85, 86-89, 238
La Sarte Monastery, 200-201
Lay Down Your Arms; see Waffen Nieder, Die
League for Peace and Freedom, 128, 129
League for Permanent Peace; see Ligue Internationale et Permanente de la Paix
League of Nations, 52, 73, 77, 81, 84, 85, 88, 89, 93, 94, 97, 110, 116, 119, 129, 137, 138, 149, 152, 170, 178, 179, 194, 206, 207, 236
LEAGUE OF THE RED CROSS SOCIETIES, 239

League of the Rights of Man, 113
Leopold II, 55
Let My People Go, 215
Lie, Trygve, 174, 219
Ligue de la Conciliation Internationale, 59
Ligue Internationale de la Paix et de la Liberté, 13
Ligue Internationale et Permanente de la Paix, 8, 9, 50, 112
Lloyd George, David, 96, 105
Locarno Pact, 97, 98, 105, 110, 132
Lombard Union, 40
London Conference (1921), 109
London Naval Conference (1908), 43
Long, John Davis, 34
Lumumba, Patrice, 220
Luther, Martin, 122
LUTHULI, CHIEF ALBERT JOHN, 208-215, 239

MacDonald, James Ramsay, 97, 140, 141
Maine, 34
Malou, Jules, 54, 55
Malthus, Thomas, 168
Mao Tze-tung, 189
MARSHALL, GEORGE C., 187-191, 239
Marshall Plan, 179, 190, 191, 218
Massey, Vincent, 194
Mobutu, Joseph, 221
MONETA, ERNESTO TEODORO, 38-41, 42, 238
Monroe Doctrine, 157
Montgomery bus boycott, 231-233
Montgomery Improvement Association (MIA), 231, 233
MOTT, JOHN R., 164-167, 239
Moynier, Gustave, 5
Münch, Eugène, 181
Mussolini, Benito, 162

NANSEN, FRIDTJOF, 90-94, 206, 238
NANSEN INTERNATIONAL OFFICE FOR REFUGEES, 94, 239
Napoleon III, 2, 4, 8, 111, 112
National Association for the Advancement of Colored People (NAACP), 230

National Defense Research Division, 225

Nature of the Chemical Bond, The, 225

New York State Legislature, 32-33

Nobel, Alfred, vii-x, 7, 27, 28, 29, 30, 87, 122

Nobel Committee, viii, 11-12, 23, 70, 85, 87, 89, 113, 142, 145, 171, 186, 204

Nobel Foundation, 203, 204

Nobel, Immanuel, ix

Nobel Institute, 87, 88

Nobel Prize in Chemistry, 226

Nobel Prize in Physics, 225

NOEL-BAKER, PHILIP J., 205-207, 239

North Atlantic Treaty Organization (NATO), 195

Norwegian-Swedish dissolution (1905), 45, 47, 48, 84, 87, 93

OFFICE OF THE UNITED NA-TIONS HIGH COMMISSION FOR REFUGEES, 239

One World Committee, 163

Organization for European Economic Cooperation (OEEC), 218, 219

OSSIETZKY, CARL VON, 143-146, 162, 227, 239

Our Slavic Fellow-Citizens, 160

Palestine, partition of, 174-175, 196-197

Paris Peace Conference, 73, 77, 81, 84, 178

Paris Peace Pact; *see* Kellogg-Briand Pact

Parliament (Belgium), 54, 72, 73

Parliament (Great Britain), 19, 21, 23, 98, 138, 140-141, 151, 207

PASSY, FRÉDÉRIC, 6, 7-10, 14, 22, 50, 51, 112, 115, 238

Patriotism Under Three Flags, 136, 137

PAULING, LINUS CARL, 223-228, 239

Pearl Harbor, 157, 189

PEARSON, LESTER BOWLES, 192-198, 239

Permanent Court of Arbitration, 23, 44, 58, 59, 63, 72, 80, 81

Permanent Court of International Justice, 120

Permanent International Peace Bureau; *see* INTERNATIONAL PEACE BUREAU

PIRE, REV. DOMINIQUE GEORGES, 199-204, 239

Portsmouth, negotiations at, 36-37

Pratt, Hodgson, 64, 72

QUIDDE, LUDWIG, 114-116, 238

Recollections of Solferino, 5

Red Cross, 5, 6, 151

Red Cross Convention of 1906, 44

Refugees as Assets, 162

Reichstag, 108

RENAULT, LOUIS, 40, 42-44, 238

Reparations Committee, 105

Research Board for National Security, 226

Review of International Law and Comparative Legislation, The, 62

Rigsdag (Denmark), 51

Riksdag (Sweden), 46, 48, 83

Roosevelt, Alice Lee, 32, 33

Roosevelt, Edith Kermit Carow, 33

Roosevelt, Franklin Delano, 148, 156, 157, 162, 189

ROOSEVELT, THEODORE, 18, 31-37, 59, 68, 69, 70, 119, 238

ROOT, ELIHU, 67-70, 238

Royal Society, 169

Ruhr, Occupation of, 109, 113

Russian Revolution, 178

Russian-Turkish War, 21, 27

Russo-Japanese War, 36

SAAVEDRA LAMAS, CARLOS, 147-149, 239

St. Laurent, Louis, 195, 198

San Francisco Conference (1945), 158, 195, 207, 216

Schrodinger, Erwin, 224, 225

SCHWEITZER, ALBERT, 180-186, 239

Schweitzer, Helene Bresslau, 183, 184

Second Women's Congress, 161

Senate (France), 59, 60, 81

245

Senate (United States), 22, 70, 77, 119, 156
Senate Internal Security Committee (United States), 227
Seventh Pan-American Conference (1933), 148, 156
Sharpeville, 214
Simon, Jules, 112
Social Demokraten, 83
Society of Friends, 206
SÖDERBLOM, NATHAN, 121-124, 166, 184, 238
Solferino, Battle of, 2, 4
Southern Christian Leadership Conference, 235
Spanish-American War, 34-35, 136
Stalin, Joseph, 157
State, The, 75
State Council (The Netherlands), 62
Storting, viii, 10, 12, 47, 48, 87, 142, 179, 228
Strassburg, University of, 114, 181, 182
STRESEMANN, GUSTAV, 97, 106, 107-110, 141, 238
Stride Toward Freedom, 234
Suez Canal Crisis, 196, 197, 207
Summerfield, Arnold, 224
Suttner, Baron Arthur von, 26, 27, 28, 30
SUTTNER, BARONESS BERTHA KINSKY VON, vii, x, 6, 7, 25-30, 65, 66, 115, 238
Swedish Academy of Science, 226
Swedish Peace and Arbitration Union, 46
Swiss Federal Council, 17

Taft, William Howard, 37, 69, 70
Tennyson, Alfred Lord, 61
Truman, Harry S., 175, 189, 190
Tshombe, Moise, 221-222

United Nations, 157, 158, 162, 163, 170, 175, 179, 195, 196, 197, 216, 218, 219-222, 227, 237
United Nations Charter, 174, 195, 207
United Nations Educational, Scientific and Cultural Organization (UNESCO), 237

United Nations General Assembly, 196, 197, 207, 219, 221
UNITED NATIONS INTERNATIONAL CHILDREN'S EMERGENCY FUND (UNICEF), 239
United Nations Relief and Rehabilitation Administration (UNRRA), 195
United Nations Security Council, 196, 197, 219
United States Congress, 22, 155
Universal Christian Conference on Life and Work, 124
Upsala, Archbishop of, 123

Versailles Conference; *see* Paris Peace Conference
Versailles, Treaty of, 108, 116

Waffen Nieder, Die (book), 29
Waffen Nieder, Die (periodical), 30, 65
Washington Disarmament Conference (1921-1922), 132
Widor, Charles Marie, 181, 182
Wilhelm II, 115
WILSON, WOODROW, 37, 74-78, 81, 129, 152, 166, 238
Women's International League for Peace and Freedom (WILPF), 125, 128, 161-162, 163
Women's Peace Party, 128
Wood, Leonard, 69
World Council of Churches, 124
World Court, 97, 120
World War I, 9, 30, 41, 44, 52, 60, 65-66, 72, 73, 76-77, 81, 84, 88, 93, 96, 100-101, 105, 106, 108, 115, 119, 123, 128, 132, 137, 141, 144, 155, 160, 162, 166, 167, 169, 177-178, 184, 188, 192-193, 196, 200, 206, 218, 225, 236
World War II, 71, 73, 138, 153, 162, 170, 179, 185, 188, 194, 196, 201, 207, 218, 220, 225, 236

Young Men's Christian Association (YMCA), 1, 165, 166, 167, 230

Zola, Émile, 112-113